For Elisa,
My best friend. I love you more than all the grains of sand!
Bobby

Extra Innings

Bobby Ezor: Ordinary Life Is Extraordinary

A few of Bobby's adventures
as told to Vince Coppola

In the summer of 2019, Karen Waksman, a dear friend, prompted me to begin the process of writing down my stories. Like life itself, it began with a simple act, a file named "Headlines." The words and memories and emotions came rushing out, the DNA of my life. This memoir contains my specific recollections of people and experiences over the last six decades. Obviously, it can't be all-encompassing—I've been blessed with many friends and want to include everyone—a virtual and physical impossibility, like counting angels on the head of a pin. Storytellers repeat themselves when they revisit relationships and past behavior. Experiences repeat themselves. Life repeats itself. And I've lived an ordinary life. If I've failed to mention you or our adventures, please know that your spirit, knowledge, and truth are very much alive on these pages. And now Karen, we're about to deliver our baby.

Table of Contents

Preface	"Fun, Fun, Fun"	7
Chapter 1	Something in the Newspaper…	13
Chapter 2	Semper Fi, Sheldon	23
Chapter 3	*Rawhide*	33
Chapter 4	Mintee Montee	39
Chapter 5	Eanelli at the Crossroads	47
Chapter 6	Hanging On for Dear Life	55
Chapter 7	Homemade Rugelach	71
Chapter 8	Zwecker Rhymes with Checker	79
Chapter 9	Accidental Wrong Turn	89
Chapter 10	Muhammad Ali and Me	97
Chapter 11	Jerry Farber's Place	111
Chapter 12	"Time is a Jet Plane…"	121
Chapter 13	Happy Trails, Coach Valentine	131
Chapter 14	Here's To You, Arnold Goodman	145
Chapter 15	Hunting for the Ultimate Truffle	153
Chapter 16	"May I Call You Bobby?"	163
Chapter 17	Uncle Bobby Meets "Frankie No"	175
Chapter 18	"Lookin' For Adventure and Whatever Comes Our Way…"	187
Chapter 19	Paterson, Sheldon's Kind of Town	195
Chapter 20	Twelve Again	203
Epilogue	"A Lovely Bunch of Guys"	213
	About the Authors	221

Preface

"Well, she got her daddy's car...

And with the radio blasting

Goes cruising just as fast as she can now...

A lotta guys try to catch her

But she leads them on a wild goose chase

now...And she'll have fun, fun, fun

'Til her daddy takes the T-bird away."

"Fun, Fun, Fun," The Beach Boys

Looking

back, it's been a great run!

I married the love of my life more than 40 years ago and we're going strong. Our children are making their way in the world. We became first-time grandparents in the tumultuous summer of 2020. I'm winding down my career as a trial lawyer—a good run—but no one will confuse me with Racehorse Haynes. I was first singles player on my high school tennis team, a decent semipro center fielder, a boxing judge, a sports agent, a Deadhead, a jack-of-all-trades. On New Year's Eve, I can still hit high G playing "Auld Lang Syne" on my clarinet. I've been the guy "with the radio blasting" since my teens—thirsty for new friendships, experiences, fresh insights, road trips, concerts, sporting events, great meals, and exotic places.

It's almost time to put the T-Bird away. My mother and father, my sister, my wife's parents—all so precious to me—have passed away. Some of my dear friends are gone, tearing a hole in the fabric of my life. Others have suffered terrible loss. Still others drifted away, pulled by life's unpredictable tides. Paterson, New Jersey—my hometown—is mostly unrecognizable to me. I hope it fires other boys' imaginations as it did my dreams of Yankee Stadium and Mickey Mantle, just across the Hudson. My father, a Marine, drilled love of country into me. I love it still, but sometimes I don't recognize it. And then comes a life-changing pandemic.

> **My Dear Children,**
>
> My friends have come to me from many walks of life. An outgoing nature initiated most; the balance, my good fortune.
> All have been good and honest people, loving and caring.
> My friends are sacred to me.
> I think of them often. I pray for them in my silent devotions.
> I care about them as I do my family. I try to force our busy schedules to intersect. Once I make a friend I don't let them go easily. I don't hold grudges. Seventy-two hours is plenty of time to get over a disagreement. In the case of immediate family, before the next sunrise (trust me on this advice). Be the bigger person where necessary. I have seen families and friendships destroyed as a result of foolish pride. I have been blessed with more than my fair share of lifelong friends. I wish the same for all of you.
>
> *Love, Dad*
>
> August 19, 2002

The Gospel according to Bobby Ezor:
"Be the bigger person where necessary."

The bible tells us "the days of our years are three score and ten." At 68, I'm approaching my expiration date. Old enough to realize "fun, fun, fun" can sour into disappointment—a wild-goose chase—if you stay too long. Recently, I've been taking a look in the rearview mirror, revisiting my experiences over the last five decades, and jotting some of them down. Calling what I've written a "memoir" is too weighty for me, but I don't believe a life well lived is "a cruise to the hamburger stand" either. I've lived and learned and regretted things, done some good along the way, never stopped caring. Often I chose paths less traveled, resisted the obvious, safe, ordinary, or mundane—and discovered that ordinary life can be extraordinary. You have to work hard, embrace humility and occasional shamelessness, and never lose your sense of humor.

I got to hang out with my childhood gods Mickey Mantle and Muhammad Ali. I made the pilgrimage "half-a-million strong" to Woodstock in 1969. At The Keystone in Berkeley, California, I almost convinced the Grateful Dead's Jerry Garcia—another of my idols—to noodle a few notes of "Happy Birthday." I stowed away on a tramp freighter bound for the Philippines and caught the "Thrilla in Manila." I have biked through sea-swept Puglia on the heel of the Italian boot, drunk Barolo wine, and hunted truffles in Tuscany. These things and others, I've shared with friends. Like my marriage, my commitment to friendship is total, seamless, and never-ending. When a beloved friend (you'll meet him in these pages) died "thin with addiction," Elisa and I welcomed his mother and daughter into our family. Twenty years later, I was honored to perform that marvelous young woman's wedding ceremony. One of the great experiences of a full life. Larry, I know you were there watching.

Hey, the radio's still blasting. I invite you join me for the ride.

Robert Ezor, February 2021

BOBBY EZOR | ORDINARY LIFE IS EXTRAORDINARY

||12||

Chapter 1

I read something in the newspaper: "Mickey Mantle is going to be passing through town." What goes on in my head: Go there!

North Georgia, 1979

I'm  hiding in the rough alongside the fairway at a plush golf course in the foothills of the Appalachian Mountains, any thought of work, responsibility, and decorum vanished from my head. I'm 27 years old, engaged to be married, and dressed head-to-toe in the pinstriped Yankees uniform I wear playing JCC softball. It's the real deal: #7 from Gerry Cosby & Co. in Manhattan, the only outlet in the country selling genuine MLB gear. I'm clutching my battered leather baseball glove, the one Grandma Bedie gave me when I was 15. Crouched next to me, wearing a pulled-down Yankees cap, is Larry Urbach, a childhood friend, now a U.S. government attorney. Larry is a hard-core Roger Maris fanboy.

After what feels like an eternity—golf is a tediously slow game—the cart comes trundling toward us. "Mickey Mantle!" I hiss to Larry. There's no mistaking him, the bulging arms, bull neck, dirty blond hair, All-American grin. Next to Mick is Kyle Rote, the New York Giants great wide receiver, and two guys I don't recognize. Mick gets out—I recognize his gimpy gait, always reminds me of Grandpa in *The Real McCoys*. Speechless, I watch him line up his putt, and then it all pours out of me: statistics, plays, and highlights. I've practically memorized his whole career—swing, hit, home run, bunt, strikeout—powerful weapons against anyone daring to claim to be the ultimate Mantle fan. "Remember that shot you hit against Chuck Stobbs? It's still going!" Of course, this is the titanic blast Mick drove off Stobbs, a rookie Washington Senators pitcher, out of Griffith Stadium, the second-longest home run in MLB history. This was 1953, when I was in diapers. By the way, Babe Ruth still holds the record for the longest.

This is the world before burly security guards and velvet ropes kept athletes and celebrities off-limits to ordinary people, a time impossible to imagine today. I shout out a few more stats. Mantle turns from the green—he's having trouble bending down to pluck his ball from the cup. I wince watching him; this is a man who endured five knee surgeries in a 17-year career.

I've definitely gotten his attention.

"What the f..k do you want!" he yells. "What are you doing here?"

"I...I just want to meet you!"

Meeting The Mick: One of those thrills of a lifetime.

"Meet me?" he shouts. "Are you a fag?"

"No, a lawyer." I nod vaguely in the direction of Yankee Stadium, a thousand miles to the north. "From up there."

"Where?"

"I've seen you play a million times," I blurt. "I...I just became a lawyer. Larry here is a lawyer too. We want to meet you. That's all."

"You two are lawyers?" He's staring at my—his uniform, at Larry's hat, at the baseball glove I'm clutching on a golf course. I can see he's bewildered, amused, and maybe a little interested.

"Come on out here."

Larry and I spill onto the manicured green, giggling like schoolkids on a playground. The two business guys, who've no doubt spent a bucket of money to play with Mantle and Rote, stare at us sourly. We introduce ourselves, make some small talk, and once again I launch into my obsession: Mantle worship. By now, I can tell Mick is getting a kick out of my routine. Only it's not a routine, it's my life.

"Look, guys," he says after a while. "I've got to play this round. Why don't you meet me at the clubhouse? We'll chat."

"Great!"

We walk back to the clubhouse, not a worry in the world. By the time Mantle and Rote arrive, a pantheon of sports gods—Pat Summerall, Roger Maris, Rocky Graziano—are laughing and goofing around in the clubhouse. After a moment, Mickey spots us. He yells to Maris and points at us, "These characters were hiding on the fairway dressed up like this." Maris looks at us and laughs. We start laughing; everybody starts laughing.

In 30 minutes we're all buddies. This is amazing. I ask Mantle to sign the thumb of my mitt and he does; Maris autographs the pinky. (I still have the glove, it's probably worth something, at least as a keepsake, but neither of my kids is interested.) The

Missing these guys: The Mick with my lifelong friend Larry Urbach.

tournament we've crashed is a charity event organized by Dan Gleason, a well-known *Golf Digest* writer. Gleason comes over to say hello. He takes in my uniform, shrugging like its standard golf attire. Gleason is a gentleman. He mentions a banquet scheduled for this evening at a midtown Atlanta hotel.

"Can you get my buddies here a couple of passes?" Mantle asks.

"Sure thing, Mick. Anything you say."

Larry has a prior commitment and begs off.

I invite Elisa, my fiancée, who's intrigued by anything from my past life (this, inevitably, will change) and call my buddy Irwin Deutsch. It won't matter what plans Irwin might have.

"Irwin, you wanna meet Mickey Mantle tonight?"

"Do I wanna meet Mickey? Are you out of your mind?"

"There's this banquet..."

"Where? When?"

On The Mick's passing, even St. Peter had to make adjustments. Cartoon by Pulitzer Prize recipient Mike Luckovich, presented to Bobby by teammate and friend Jay Smith, publisher of The Atlanta Journal-Constitution.

Elisa, now my wife of 41 years, is soft-spoken, intelligent, and gracious. Irwin, who sadly passed away in 2019, is boorish, obstreperous, a know-it-all who can't bring himself to speak below a shout. A 300-pound wrecking ball catapulted out of the Lower East Side of Manhattan to Atlanta. I love him. He's the only person I've ever known whose encyclopedic knowledge of Mantle approaches mine. Our first meeting, in an apartment complex parking lot, quickly devolved into a spitting contest to determine who possessed more Mantle trivia. He spit on my shoe to make a point. I spit on the windshield of his car, an improvement because it was a rolling garbage scow. Of course, we became great friends, a bond that Elisa and most of our friends, never fully understood.

We arrive at the Colony Square Hotel in midtown Atlanta. Irwin, who mostly looks like an unmade bed, is wearing a jacket in honor of Mantle; Elisa, a clingy red and grey number that turns heads. Given my age and profession, I'm still innocent about my idols. Part of it is hero worship—I've been fixated on Mick since I was eight years old—but there's a tradition among sports reporters to whitewash famous athletes' personal "issues" that goes at least as far back as Babe Ruth. I must have been 18 when I read pitcher Jim Bouton's best-selling *Ball Four* exposé, but his depiction of Mantle as a hard-drinking party animal flew right over my head. Mickey is about to set me straight.

As we walk in, he spots us from the dais.

"Hey, here's the lawyer!" Mantle shouts, staggers to his feet, and lurches over.

"You showed up!"

"Are you kidding? Thank you!" I gush.

I introduce Elisa adding, "We recently got engaged." Next to me, Irwin is grinning like a 10-year-old.

"Can I kiss the bride?" Mickey asks, stepping closer. I'm reminded of Dean Martin's notorious drunk routines.

"That's up to her."

"Yes," says Elisa smiling, "You can kiss the bride!"

He moves quickly for his bulk, sweeps her into his arms, puts her into a big dip, and plants one on her lips. Then he sticks his tongue down her throat.

"Can I kiss the bride?"

I'm standing there. When he finally releases her, I hesitate as if uncertain, then grab him by the lapels—he reeks of alcohol—and with a straight face say, "Anybody but you, I'd punch right in the nose!" He looks at me, glassy-eyed, uncertain, then I add, "But it's you. I may not let her brush her teeth for a week!"

"WHAT ARE YOU A FAGGOT?" he shouts. (It's a theme with this guy.) We're half-serious, half-laughing. I turn to Elisa and say sotto voce, "And you, you didn't have to close your eyes!"

Mantle and I get into this preposterous back and forth until he staggers back to the dais. I can see he's having a hard time staying awake, but every now and then, he looks up, eyeballs us, and waggles his tongue. I crack up. He grins and puts his head in the soup. It doesn't get any better as the affair grinds on, but somehow he pulls himself together.

"What are ya'll doing tonight?" he asks.

"Whatever you're doing."

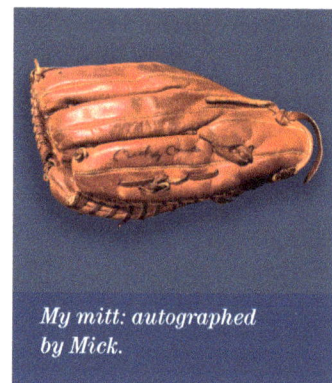

My mitt: autographed by Mick.

"You know the bars around here?"

"Some."

I've gone from uninvited guest to ringleader.

In the 1970s, the Atlanta bar scene is wild, a nonstop party fueled by rock and roll, sex, drugs, sports, youth, and celebrity. Legions of young people—Black, white, gay, straight, single, divorced—escaped the dreary routines of small-town life for the glitz and glitter of "Hotlanta." Irwin, Mickey, Kyle Rote, Pat Summerall, Rocky Graziano, Elisa, and I, along with a woman I discover is Mantle's "minder," make our way to Harrison's, a cavernous singles palace on Peachtree Street not far from the hotel. It takes a while—Atlanta is not New York—but a buzz builds and soon everyone is staring, grinning, and waving hello, the bolder women coming over, eager for a taste of celebrity. I order a round of drinks—Mickey downs vodka martinis like lemonade—and wave for more. When he's not looking, I dump mine under the table. Irwin is doing some crazy shit. He knows each of these athletes' careers intimately and starts saying things that nobody would ever say to them. He gets into a hilarious "dese and dose" exchange with Rocky, mimicking the fighter's gestures and speech word for word. Graziano, a little punchy, gets a kick out of it. He asks Irwin, "Did you actually see Mickey play?"

"Did I see Mickey play?" Irwin shouts. "I've seen Mantle bat more times than he's been up!"

Mantle is howling. He loves Irwin. Graziano loves Irwin. They all love Irwin. They're mesmerized, as if some mad guru spouting statistics and highlights has sprung up out of the earth. Of course, this is not enough for Irwin. Nothing is ever enough. I look around and he's vanished. No, he's under the table. He's rolled up Mantle's pant legs. He's tracing the scars from the surgeries. Mickey is letting him do it.

"What are you doing man?" I hiss.

"These are Mickey's surgeries," Irwin says. Awestruck, as if he's found a holy relic among the peanut shells, fries, and spilled beer.

My mitt: autographed by Maris.

"I'm touching Mickey's surgeries."

"You're out of your f..king mind!"

The evening winds down with Mantle blindly throwing wads of cash around to cover the tab. The minder, who's no doubt seen it all before, scoops some of his dough back up to keep him from ripping himself off. Am I embarrassed to see my lifelong idol in this sorry state? Do I lament how far the mighty have fallen? Are you kidding? It's the opposite. It's magical. Irwin and I are privileged to see the great Mickey Mantle and his band of brothers, these incomparable athletes and legends—all gone now—alive and raising hell. It wasn't a one-night stand either.

Mickey, his wife Merlyn, and I will meet again over the next decades. I invite him to my wedding and the Mantles graciously send Elisa and me a wedding present. I still have it along with my baseball mitt.

Chapter 2

Semper Fi, Sheldon

A Marine on the March: Sheldon D. Ezor moving up the corporate ladder. Sheldon Ezor and Jack Lubke (president, Encyclopedia Americana). Dad as a Marine. Dad receives Americana Man of the Year award from Grolier Society Chairman of the Board F.P. Murphy, 1953.

California Ezors: Dad's half-brother Raymond Ezor with Great Uncle Albert Ezor and Great Uncle William Ezor. Dad's 80th with me at Barclays Center in Brooklyn. Visiting Aunt Sylvia and Uncle Al out west.

L.A. cousin Gary Ezor (owner of The Pioneer Broach Co.) with Bobby and Dad's half-brother Raymond. Dad and Uncle Al. Dad's half-brother Raymond and my mom Estelle Ezor.

Teen Adventures: Bobby (15 years old) with dad's half-brother Raymond. Bobby aboard Uncle Al's boat in Marina Del Ray, California. My mother's first car, a 1957 Chevy Bel Air. Bobby speaking in Dad's Dress Blues at Barnsley Gardens in Adairsville, Georgia, 2005.

My  father wasn't home a lot.

He was working, this bull of a man who came out of the Depression and World War II determined to prove himself. Like fellow Marine and syndicated columnist Art Buchwald, Sheldon Ezor credited the Corps for the discipline and can-do determination that would make him successful; though, of course, other forces were at work. At 17, Buchwald ran away from a Hebrew orphanage, convinced a vagrant—a pint of rotgut whiskey played a part—to pose as his father and sign his enlistment papers. At the same age, my dad journeyed halfway across the country to convince his estranged father to allow him to sign up. After the war, denied admission to NYU's dental school ("Jews don't have the right hands for dentistry," one dental school dean insisted at the time), Sheldon recalibrated.

A lean-mean fighting machine: Sheldon Ezor, Parris Island, Port Royal, South Carolina, 1944.

Back in his hometown of Paterson, New Jersey, with a pregnant wife and an infant daughter in tow, Sheldon took a dead-end job at Stenchever's, the city's upscale department store. A natural salesman and inveterate hondler, he convinced Harold Stenchever to add a line of accessories—matching handbags, gloves, belts—a big success. Instead of the promotion Sheldon had earned, Stenchever fired him and gave the job to one of his sons. "Blood is thicker than water," my father explained to me many years later. He kept a supply of adages that he used to explain life's challenges, twists, and disappointments. "Everything in moderation," he'd say. Or when referring to me, his wayward son, "The apple doesn't fall very far from the tree." Then he'd add meaningfully, "...unless the tree is planted on a very steep hill."

Sheldon was already attacking the next hill. At Stenchever's, he'd disappear on his lunch hour, reappear in one of the Main Street banks, and emerge clutching a roll of dimes. He scanned the birth announcements of the *Paterson Evening News* and spent his break in a phone booth making cold calls. When he got lucky, which was often—who could deny a newborn baby the promise of an education?—he'd make the parents an offer they couldn't refuse: Grolier Inc.'s *The Book of Knowledge* or the *Encyclopedia Americana*, with a "handsome bookcase in your choice of finishes" thrown in, and the option of paying "on time."

A little R&R: Dad and Mom (forefront) with Dad's cousins Leonard and Betty Blumenfeld (right) and friends Bill and Ettie Feldman (left) at the Plaza, 1943.

In postwar America, the encyclopedia, like the car and color TV, is the sine qua non of middle-class aspirations. Every family had to have a set. Sheldon would sell these books, market them, and train others to sell them, a career path he'd follow for the rest of his life. At Grolier Inc., he rose from salesman, to manager, to vice president, and then to national sales coordinator. One of my earliest memories is driving to work with my father. On a good day, we could leave Paterson and be in Midtown Manhattan in 35 minutes. To a kid, Grolier Americana's headquarters was this "golden skyscraper" on 34th Street. When I look back, the vibe was right out of *Mad Men*. We'd pass through the doors and this voluptuous receptionist in stiletto heels and tight skirt would wiggle up to greet us. One time, company president Jack Lubke caught me staring.

"Robert, what do you think of that?" he winked.

"Think of what?" I answered.

A few years later, when Lubke promoted one of his rivals for a top job at Grolier, Sheldon quit—no easy thing—and built a very robust educational publishing company of his own.

My father struggled with abandonment issues his whole life, a wound he stubbornly refused to acknowledge. As a child, living with his immigrant grandparents and divorced mother, he'd fight to run every errand and fix anything in the house that was broken. As an adult, he yearned to reconnect with his father, half-brother, and the Los Angeles branch of our family, but could never bring himself to do so.

At 15, I'd already embraced my "no such thing as a wrong turn" philosophy: I went AWOL from a Santa Monica Boulevard hotel. My sister and I were on a cross-country "teen tour" and I called Aunt Anita, who in turn called my amazing Aunt Sylvia (Uncle Al's wife), who arranged for me to spend a couple of wonderful days with the California Ezors—uncles, aunts, and cousins I'd never met. When I got back to Jersey, my father sat me down on the porch one Sunday morning, thirsting for information.

"What does my half-brother look like?" he asked.

"Where does my father live?"

"Did he show you around?"

"Sure!"

"Where'd you go?"

"The Brown Derby...the Hollywood Bowl."

"Wow!"

Dad always said there were two ways to win a tug-of-war: "Pull 'em over to your side or let go of the rope." Sheldon (second in line) as a freshman at NYU, 1942.

Many years later, I learned that Archie Ezor, my dad's father, struggled as the rest of the family flourished. Archie's brother, Albert, the patriarch, owned a broaching company that did very fine machine work, so fine he won a number of NASA contracts. I visited the sleek sailboat Albert kept docked at Marina del Rey with Ray Ezor, my father's half-brother, a man my dad had never met and would never get to know. Another Ezor grew a scrap metal operation, long a mainstay of immigrant entrepreneurs, into a very profitable business. Meanwhile, my grandfather Archie hustled pool to make a living. Family legend has it he once beat Minnesota Fats. That I liked.

When Sheldon Met Estelle.

Mom and Dad at the Copacabana in NYC, 1955.

Sheldon was shipping out to the Pacific when he met Estelle Preblud at a USO dance in Providence, and though smitten, he lost her contact information. He'd later claim the scrap of paper he jotted her address on was in his uniform pocket when he dropped off his laundry. From the Mariana Islands—8,000 miles from Rhode Island—he convinced a stateside Marine to track down "this pretty freckle-faced girl" and get her mailing address, an impulse that led to my sister's and my existence and their 70-odd year marriage.

Wedding anniversaries were always celebrated as if our house was Buckingham Palace and we were in Queen Elizabeth II's entourage: "My Dear, on this the 50th (fill in the number) anniversary of our wedding," Dad would proclaim, "I can honestly say it's been 41 of the most wonderful years of my life." So part of his salesman's shtick; so corny and so familiar that my mom, my sister, and I would recite the words along with him.

Estelle Preblud's family fled Russia and its pogroms for the safe harbor of Providence, Rhode Island. Estelle was beautiful and gifted, with a soprano so enthralling a music teacher arranged for her to audition at the Julliard School of Music. Accepted, she began the long commute into Manhattan, a first step toward a career beyond her wildest imagining. Her father, "Bill" (Wolf) Preblud, was a fruit peddler who read the *Jewish Forverts (Forward)*, "the voice of the Jewish immigrant and the conscience of the ghetto," religiously. A romance between a smooth-talking hondler from New Jersey and his gifted daughter might have sounded like a storyline lifted from Yiddish theater. Ever the salesman, Sheldon put his future father-in-law's suspicions at ease ("What, a blue-eyed autseyder courting my daughter?"). He read the *Forverts* to Wolf in Yiddish.

Sheldon and Estelle were already in love. On his return from the Pacific, Sheldon was promoted to drill sergeant and ordered to report to the sprawling Marine Corps base on Parris Island. The two married in a small ceremony in Beaufort, South Carolina, 10 miles from the base. Bob Adler, the Jewish Marine who'd tracked down Estelle's Providence address, was the best man.

In 1955, when I was three years old, our family moved into a spacious English Tudor in Paterson's leafy Eastside Park neighborhood, an indicator of my father's burgeoning career success. In the postwar years, men were breadwinners; women homemakers. Feminism, women's liberation, and two-career families were at least a generation away. To my knowledge, other than a wartime stint in a munitions plant, my mother never held a job, but she never stopped working—cooking and cleaning and raising two kids while my father was busy making money.

Our house in Paterson: Ironically, the Pinks lived next door.

Not long after Grandfather Preblud died, Grandma Sadie, my mom's mother, came to live with us. She stayed 35 years. Sadie was wise and gentle and understood firsthand what was important in life. Unlike my parents—maybe everyone's parents—who had a simplified notion of "success," my mellow Yiddish Bubbe accepted me as I was. Her thick accent was comforting, a connection to Europe and a larger world than Jersey. She'd bake the most delicious apple pies—and slip me a few bucks to play poker with my friends.

When we moved to our new house, Dad brought in a live-in housekeeper named Lois to help out. Over the years, two other Southern Black women lived with us. I bonded with all of them: Lois stayed until I was seven; in my kid's mind, she made the best fried chicken imaginable. Then came Virginia, a behemoth of a woman who'd run around in lavender-colored panties. She taught me how to play poker and board games. When I came of age there was Della from South Carolina. As a college student, I was far less comfortable having Black "help" serving us. I clashed with my mother—and no doubt embarrassed Della—when I insisted she take her meals in the dining room with us. This led to a late-night summit meeting between my parents.

They eventually agreed with me.

The housekeepers lived in our "maids' quarters," a finished attic with two bedrooms and a full bath. (Something I wouldn't see again until I relocated to Georgia.) At the time, my mother's close friends Ettie Feldman and Frieda Marshall (and who knows how many others) were doing the same. A housekeeper was a symbol of the good life, the American Dream, North Jersey style.

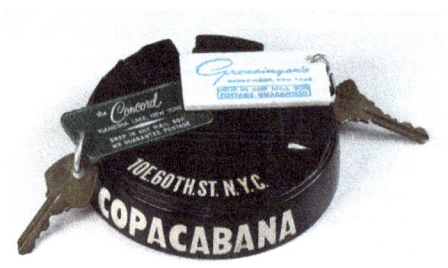

Sheldon's Souvenirs: Copacabana ashtray and room keys from the Borscht Belt.

Mom pampered me. She wanted me to "taste everything, open my eyes, and live." She'd spot the great entertainers and point them out to me. With my father always gone and my sister struggling with developmental issues, I became her "everything." She insisted that my father take me places I probably never would have seen. Sheldon take a 12-year-old to the Copacabana? He didn't need that. They'd schmear the guy at the front and sneak me in. We went to the Catskills several times a summer, sometimes just for dinner and a show. I recall seeing Steve Lawrence and Eydie Gorme, Jerry Lewis and Shecky Greene. As I grew older and inevitably started to pull away, Mom became unsettled. She had abandonment issues of her own.

My mother was outgoing, social, and very fashionable. She held credit accounts with the finest Manhattan department stores—her charges drove my father to distraction. When she threw a party, she planned it down to the last detail. She loved interior design and furnished my room as if I were Napoleon on the Isle of Elba. She never tracked household expenses. My father overlooked that. She never helped us with our homework. I could do the work but my sister needed help. Dad was the guy. Mom didn't drive until I was five. "You have to learn!" my father lectured. He gave her driving lessons in the Dunkin' Donuts parking lot every Sunday. And when she got her license, he bought her a new '57 Chevy Bel Air, pink with very cool brushed steel panels on the rear fenders.

She was curious, very empathetic, and had a great heart. But over time, her brief moment at Julliard must have seemed like silver pieces of someone else's life, a glimmer of what might have been. After I left for college and Grandma Sadie passed away, she grew terribly lonely and insecure. Decades later, she was distraught that she didn't get to Atlanta often enough to see Zack, her first grandchild, her "little Zeckie."

She wanted to raise me all over again.

I never gave her credit. Now that I'm in the last quarter of my life, I realize so much of my personality and my tastes come from my mother. My father? He'd eat whatever was put in front of him. He'd wear his boxer shorts until they were in tatters, drove a Lincoln only because its roomy front seat better supported his expanding bulk. As for my career choices, he would have preferred me enlisting in the Marine Corps.

Mom and Dad dance at my Bar Mitzvah, 1965.

And yet, this marriage of opposites was a lifelong love affair. There's a lesson here—I'm not sure what it is, but I want to emulate it, want my children to appreciate it. I'm the child of both parents. I loved them both desperately and differently. And yet, it was my father I'd missed growing up; the father I'd yearn to see pull up in our driveway; the father who'd take me for burgers on the weekends; the father who'd guided my way into the temple that would be one of the pillars of my adult life: Yankee Stadium.

BOBBY EZOR | ORDINARY LIFE IS EXTRAORDINARY

Chapter 3

"Rollin,' rollin,' rollin,' Rawhide…Rawhide."

Rawhide, 1959–1966 TV series

A friendship that has lasted a lifetime: Bobby and Danny through the years.

My first 26-inch Schwinn (now hanging in my man cave). My mom and Danny's mom Sylvia Lawrence. Boyhood friends David Brawer, Michael Krugman, Barry Spector, Bobby, and Danny Lawrence, 1965. Bobby and Danny in '40s garb.

Danny on his first ten-speed. Danny with his first car, a 1970 VW Beetle, circa 1975. Bobby and Danny on a bike trip in the Northeast. My sister Susan Ezor escorts me in my "stagecoach"; word has it Danny was being strolled right next to me in his carriage, 1954. Me and Danny with my restored 1960 Schwinn Corvette.

Bobby, 1974. Danny, 1974. Clockwise Elisa Ezor, Danny Lawrence, Sylvia Lawrence, Bobby, Zachary Ezor, and Aaron Jacobowitz. Danny toasts to the memories. Danny on a fully restored Schwinn banana seat (he was on the cutting edge).

I'm two years old.

Danny Lawrence, my oldest friend, is beside me in a baby carriage as big as a stagecoach. In my memory, *Rawhide's* theme song is always playing as we rumble across the prairie.

That can't be right.

We're being pushed—I'm told—by our grannies, both named Sadie. This is Eastside Park, a lush turn-of-the-century greenspace haunted by the ghosts of Paterson's vanished elite. As I grow older, the 66-acre park—with its cricket pitch, baseball and football fields, tennis courts, hitching posts, ornamental pagodas, Civil War artillery, Columbus and Pulaski statues, and caged deer—transforms into a Coney Island of fantasies and imaginary westerns. Its hedges and hidden bowers are a garden of earthly delights where my first fumbling, incense-fueled adolescent sexual encounters unfolded. On clear nights, the lights of Manhattan beckon in the distance.

As kids, Danny and I talk about stuff we can't share with anyone else. His parents are heading toward a painful divorce, a rare thing in the 1950s. I'm orphaned by my father's 24/7 career, a common thing. My mother is so protective I'm smothered. Sylvia, Danny's mother, is a woman of great empathy and awareness. His father is a surgeon who drives a hot rod Pontiac GTO; my workaholic father has a Lincoln Town Car. We roam freely in each other's houses, taking the best of each other's lives and routines: traditional meals served in the dining room of my house; Sunday morning breakfasts at Danny's house, a space filled with books and newspapers and three-dimensional replicas of Andy Warhol's avant-garde soup cans, where his overachieving brothers argue politics and current events. Danny and I bone up on anatomy by thumbing through the pages of Dr. Lawrence's *Playboy* collection.

We're both escape artists: Danny builds painstakingly perfect model cars and planes in his room; I'm focused on my clarinet; both of us love my father's collection of big band music. I'm obsessed with Mickey Mantle, my Peter Pan in a line of magical heroes. We race slot cars at Danny's. At the Jersey Shore, we walk the boardwalks, checking out the girls and the concerts, and we battle "gigantic" ocean waves. In winter, we shovel snow until icicles form on our brows. We tell ourselves we want to earn a few bucks, but it's really the blizzard of honest, earnest conversation—music...politics...girls...Johnny Carson's *Tonight Show* monologues—that bonds our friendship. Danny vouches for me with the rowdy crew that hangs out in Paul Arrington's "attic." We smoke our first cigarettes, drink beer, display our "protection," i.e., never-to-be-used Trojans.

We're bicycle buddies—an escape we avail ourselves of to this day—packing peanut butter and jelly sandwiches and apples in our "saddlebags." We ride 26 miles north to Tallman, New York, and back. Danny has carefully mapped the route, allowing us to avoid potholes, busy highways, and heavily trafficked roads. I'm on my red three-speed Schwinn Corvette with chrome fenders and handbrakes; Danny, a Schwinn American. We leave early in the morning and get back just before sunset, our parents none the wiser.

When you're young, you believe best friends are forever. But life happens. On a lark, I apply to the sprawling University of Maryland outside Baltimore. Danny attends Nasson in Maine and later, Beloit in Wisconsin, small liberal arts colleges. I move to Atlanta, attend law school, and somehow convince Elisa Zwecker to marry me. Time passes. Danny never marries. His brothers move on and away. The eldest, David, is a political science professor and die-hard Pirates fan. Bookish Johnny who tattooed my skull with noogies when I was a kid, becomes Nancy Pelosi's chief of staff.

In his twenties, Danny spends summers biking in Germany, masters the language, makes like-minded biking friends, and becomes an incredibly capable rider. I'm not part of this world, but I'm happy for him. As a kid, Danny was a loner, never part of the rowdy, sports-driven outdoor life that took root in Eastside Park, a trait that intensifies over time. He has never allowed another human being to drive one of his cars or ride his bicycles—except me—and only on rare occasions. He missed the cell phone revolution. When he gets a phone, he doesn't check messages, and even today, rarely texts. Our old friends, who love him, are forever pissed off at his behavior.

I'm not. If anything, as an adult I've been able to start directing our paths to make them intersect. We've taken some incredible trips, one to Martha's Vineyard. Danny complains but always shows up. A bike trip to Montreal in 2020 didn't happen, but it took a pandemic to derail it. Soon, I suspect, age, another kind of virus, will make that impossible. My red Schwinn Corvette, the same bike I rode to Tallman, is in my garage ready to get back on the highway. Danny and I restored it.

I understand him. I'd like to think Danny understands me. We're Siamese twins joined together in those long-ago baby carriages, separated by vastly different lives and circumstances, with personalities that could not be more different, and yet, always and forever, connected.

Chapter 4

"Mintee Montee! Mintee Montee is Up!"

Grandma Sadie, my Yiddish Bubbe

It's always Saturday morning.

Channel 11 is always tuned in on the outsized black-and-white TV in the den. Officer Joe Bolton, a weatherman wearing a NYPD uniform, delights me with the Depression-era antics of *Little Rascals*, *Three Stooges*, and *Popeye the Sailor Man*. On Saturdays, WPIX, an independent television station, airs *Dick Tracy*, *Bozo the Clown*, Hollywood reruns, and, if memory serves, a cheesy wrestling show teasing the evening card at Madison Square Garden. My father is upstairs in his office paying bills, trying to figure out how he and his team can sell even more of the hefty Grolier encyclopedias that guarantee my mom, my sister, and I never want for anything. This is suburban, baby-boomer America at its most pure and innocent, before Vietnam, Nixon, and the Rolling Stones.

A sports nut, Dad takes me to my first Yankees game in 1955 and changes my life forever. I was three years old and I still remember the field—that startling emerald green—coming into view as we walked to our seats. To this day, a baseball field is a very beautiful sight (I've built one in my backyard). I'll never forget the roar of the crowd when a Yankees batter—number 7 emblazoned on his back—blasted a monster home run into the stands, and trotted like a young god around the bases. Later, when baseball stats and stories become legend to my friends and me, I learn (my father kept the program) the batter who hit the homer that clinched that long-ago game against the Washington Senators (4–2) was Mickey Mantle.

I'm enamored at five.

At six, I can keep box scores.

By eight, I'm madly in love. I'm hopping around, counting the minutes until Mel Allen's lilting, mesmerizing drawl carries me away like one of Peter Pan's *Lost Boys* to Yankee Stadium, that never-never land of the Bronx. I believe the Yankees live in the stadium, that Casey Stengel is their grandfather, and that I'm part of the family. On Saturday afternoons, Andy Pink, our neighbors' teenage son, shoots baskets in his backyard, a scene surely repeated all over America. Envious, I watch him from our second-floor window. One Saturday, I head downstairs and duck through the hedge into his yard for a closer look. Andy, a good guy, agrees to teach me some basketball basics, dribbling, layups, and foul shots.

Mintee Montee: Bobby and Yiddish Grandma Sadie, 1953.

Wait, my obsession! The Yankees game is about to start on Channel 11.

Grandma Sadie is from Rhode Island, but she grew up in Russia, the Russia of pogroms and Cossacks, starvation and persecution. She speaks mostly Yiddish with a few bits of mangled Russian and English thrown in. She loves me madly and understands I have this mysterious role model whose name, for the life of her, she can't pronounce.

"Mintee Montee!" is as close as she gets.

A clever fellow with a career in the law ahead of me, I come up with a workable solution: "Bubbe, when you hear Mel Allen say, 'Now in the on-deck circle, the great Mickey Mantle!' open the window and yell!"

I return to Andy Pink's backyard basketball clinic.

"Raahbert! Mintee Montee is up! Mintee Montee!"

Instantly, I drop the ball, duck through the hedge, run up the backstairs to the den, just in time to see Mickey step up to the plate. I glue myself to the TV. Over the years, we repeat this ritual hundreds of times. Grandma Sadie gets a kick out of what must seem to her an incomprehensible game.

My father is my first hero, but he's not around. I sit by the window every evening between 5:00 and 7:00 p.m., hoping against hope he'll show up. He rarely does. I see him on weekends, but not a whole lot of him. I have no brothers, no male cousins other than a couple out-of-towners I see maybe once a year. I have good friends. My sister loves me desperately, but she has

The Gambler: Bobby playing cards at Camp Braybank, 1959.

developmental issues she'll struggle with the rest of her life. Mickey is with me 24/7. I never miss an at bat if I can help it; never miss a game on TV, on the radio, at my sleepaway camp in the Poconos. I have a transistor radio in my bunk so I hear Red Barber, another Southerner, calling Mantle's swings, hits, misses, homers, strikeouts through the static, fading in and out in the night. It's calming, as if all is well in a turbulent world and nuclear war is not on the horizon.

Mantle is the all-American boy, the perfect ballplayer, natural, innocent, and pure. He chews bubble gum playing center field, so I chew bubble gum. I study how he blows his bubbles, how he flips his batting helmet. I never know he's flawed; they keep it quiet. I never think about what he means to me psychologically—what kid does?—he just gives me joy. The Yankees are in the World Series seven times between 1957 and 1965, my formative years. They're always in the World Series, so there must be thousands, maybe millions, of kids like me.

I crave some kind of heroic figure. Mickey Mantle, from the day he hits that home run in 1955, is planted in my head...the whole place stands up in ovation. Yankee

Stadium, all sky and steel and emerald grass, gesticulating men in fedoras, organ crescendos, and the smell of spilled beer and perfume is reduced in my five-year-old mind to a roar.

Grandma Sadie at my wedding, 1979.

Over time, my father begins to sense this. In his literal Marine Corps mind, I've gone overboard. It's his duty to haul me back in. Our back-and-forth over Mantle injuries and declining skills goes on for years. By 1968, the Yankees are a shell of the old Bronx Bombers, but I'm still clinging to a Mick now in his twilight. My father razzes me with some nonsense that Mantle can't hold Yankees outfielder Tom Tresh's jockstrap. A switch-hitter and Golden Glove winner, Tresh is the American League Rookie of the Year in 1962.

On May 30, 1968, Dad and his business partner, Les Benowitz, take me to the first game of a midweek doubleheader. I'm 16, and full of myself.

Dad: "Robert, today, we see for ourselves who's the better ballplayer."

Mantle homers in his first at bat.

Dad: "Anyone can get lucky one time."

Mantle drives a double to right center field. Tresh draws a walk.

Dad: "Tresh's eye is that good."

Mantle follows with a single, another towering homer, and a double. He goes 5-for-5.

This is Mantle's final season. The last time I see him play in person, though we will meet again.

Driving over the majestic George Washington Bridge that links New York City to the New Jersey Palisades, Dad, still trying to rein me in, asks out of the blue, "If we're driving to Yankee Stadium and Mickey Mantle is in the lane right next to us, and we both get a flat at the same time, whose tire would you help fix?"

Without missing a beat, I say, "Are you nuts? I can change your tire anytime!"

Many years later, my father, now in the grip of old age, is honored by some Jersey civic or charitable organization—he was always the big joiner. Elisa and I fly up to attend the ceremony. We give him a gift commemorating the event, a glass-blown Frabel sculpture representing Victory. I write a letter telling my father how proud I am of him, what an honor it's been to be his son. At the end, I add,

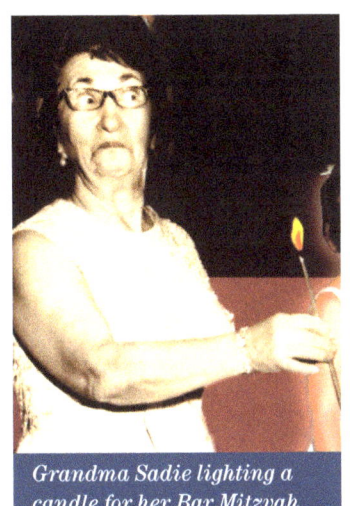

Grandma Sadie lighting a candle for her Bar Mitzvah boy, 1965.

"I would have changed your tire first."

He looks at me and nods.

He remembers.

Chapter 5

"I came to a crossroads."

Thomas "Buddy" Eanelli

I'm

15. I work for Ms. Katie McCabe.

McCabe is my fantasy of Billy Wilder's *The Front Page* come to life. The no-nonsense, chain-smoking, caffeine-addled driving force behind *The Crite's* (Eastside High School *Criterion*) outstanding performances at the Columbia Scholastic Press Association's annual competitions.

High School Band Director Thomas Eanelli aka Buddy Neal.

I'm the sports editor, hard-charging too, like my idols Mantle and Cassius Clay. I get an idea for a short feature to break up the monotony of covering too many strikeouts and missed jump shots: "Sports Spotlight," a profile of a sports personality at Eastside High School.

"Good idea. Run with it," McCabe says.

I choose Thomas Eanelli, a music teacher. A stretch, but Eanelli leads the Eastside Ghosts marching band—I'm the clarinet player—that high-steps its way to Hinchliffe Stadium for the football team's annual Turkey Game against crosstown rival John F. Kennedy High School. A good-looking guy who's put on some serious weight over the seasons, Eanelli literally stops the parade in front of his Italian in-laws' bakery on Main Street for a thumping performance of their favorite song, "Grenada." Mr. Eanelli uses the few minutes we take to play the song to catch his breath, and we march on.

I pitch him as a profile. To my delight, he agrees.

Our first interview is in the bandroom. He sits on his high-top padded stool, arms resting on the music stand. At some point, he mentions he's moonlighting at a piano bar on McBride Avenue, in Totowa, a working-class neighborhood in west Paterson.

"Great." I'll need some "color" to brighten my story.

"Dad, Mr. Eanelli is playing at this bar."

Dad knows every note of every big band song of his era. Intrigued, he drives me—I can't get in without him—to the Three Sisters, a bar that under various owners dates back to 1933 when Prohibition ended. It's dark and smoky; there's Buddy at the piano, a guy I know only from the oompah of the marching band, playing jazz. I've been to the Copa and seen a lot of Catskills stuff, but this is the first time I've been this close to a musician who is really at another level. Eanelli is improvising, his pudgy little fingers going so fast I can barely follow, firing off notes and chords and trills. I'm mesmerized and when the melody finally comes around I'm standing there grinning, well, like a 15-year-old.

All the News that Fits: Journalism teacher Katie McCabe and boyhood friends and fellow Criterion *staff members (left to right) Doug Kurtz, Steve Steinberg, Teddy Woolruch, Danny Lawrence, Bobby and Barry Spector, 1969.*

I love this guy.

We talk a little during his breaks. No one is here for avant-garde music. The bar makes money when Eanelli plays requests and customers buy him drinks. Simple as that. I notice he's glassy-eyed.

When I put it all together, Eanelli's story is staggering: a handsome Italian kid from Paterson; a player so good he competes at the Newport Jazz Festival; so good he becomes jazz singer Peggy Lee's accompanist and tours the country with her. As we're talking in the music room, he plays a few bars of "Fever," Lee's scorching sexual anthem, on the blond upright piano.

"You give me fever…"

And then, he continues: "I came to a crossroads. I met my wife and we settled down." There are tears in his eyes over what might have been. I love this guy.

I spend hours writing the story. It begins, "Right here under our noses is a great musician..." I rush it to Katie McCabe, who, as usual, is in her basement cave with her *New York Times* and Mr. Coffee machine.

She reads it (too quickly I'm thinking).

"It's good work," she says, "but I'm gonna pass."

"What! Why?" I've just learned what being "invested" in something means.

"Because I said so."

Could she have said that?

"Get going, Robert. You need to fill that space."

"I'm not going to walk out without a reason."

"Yes, you are."

"I quit!" I was always hasty with the "I quits."

When I get home, the argument with Katie McCabe is playing over and over in my head. Of course, my father picks that moment to ask about my day.

"I did this. I did that. (long pause) I quit *The Crite*."

"What did you say?"

If I'm expecting him to take my side, to share my outrage, I couldn't be more wrong. The U.S. Marine drill sergeant makes an appearance.

"Robert, we're going to get up early tomorrow morning and go back there and you are going to apologize to Ms. McCabe. And beg for your job!"

"Not that important."

"Yes it is. You're going to be applying to colleges. This is gonna be on your resume. You don't realize it now, but these little things are going to be the difference if you get into this school or not."

Now comes the lecture: I'm "wet behind the ears...Who do I think I am being so disrespectful?"

"I'm not wrong here."

"Yes, you are."

"Why?"

"Because I said so!"

The next morning, hating every step, I walk down to *The Crite* office, my father marching beside me.

Sheldon: "Katherine, Robert has something to say."

Me: "So-rry."

Sheldon: "Sorry for what? And what else!"

Me: "Sorry for being disrespectful. I'd like my job back."

McCabe: "I can't just give you your job back. What will the rest of the staff think?"

So on top of everything, I'm demoted to associate editor, effectively ending my journalism career. Buddy Eanelli, who played with Peggy Lee, Mel Torme, and Gene Krupa, will die of a heart attack a few years later at age 48.

I return to Eastside High while I'm at the University of Maryland. I visit Katie McCabe. To my surprise, she tells me she's troubled by the Eanelli incident. She tells me there was more to the story than Buddy let on. He quit the road because his Paterson girlfriend, later his wife, was pregnant. McCabe was hoping to avoid bringing renewed attention and further embarrassment to what at the time was a scandal. The world was a much simpler place back then.

Best wishes, Buddy Eanelli.

All this is years before Joe Clark, the bat-wielding principal portrayed by Morgan Freeman in *Lean On Me*, arrives at the school. Despite the Hollywood boost, Clark's much ballyhooed reforms did not take root. When last I checked, as the Covid-19 virus was cresting in the spring of 2020, Eastside High was in the bottom 10 percent of New Jersey's 300-plus high schools.

BOBBY EZOR | ORDINARY LIFE IS EXTRAORDINARY

Chapter 6

I'm hanging on for dear life and Larry's galloping, whipping the horses, and flying down the beach. Next thing I know, I'm lying in a pile of sand.

Eleuthera Island, 1978

Summer

1969. I pull up to the high-rise dorm, my blue-and-white Buick Skylark packed with clothes; pillows; sheets; a desk lamp; my Motown, Grateful Dead, and Beatles albums; a few books—not much else other than Sheldon Ezor's Sunoco credit card. The drive south from Paterson takes four hours, and if I have any deep thoughts about leaving home, or my future, or spending the next four years at the sprawling University of Maryland campus south of Baltimore, I don't remember them.

I do have a vague notion of dental school; no doubt planted in my head when my mom takes my sister to the orthodontist. She notices that Dr. Mann drives a very nice car. "You need to be an orthodontist!" she decrees. I don't have any love for dentists, dentistry, the sciences, or even Maryland. I've applied to 13 colleges, but decide on College Park when I learn the very bright Scott Kessler, one of my high school classmates, is headed here. Today, Kessler is a renowned NYC otolaryngologist whose patients include Mariah Carey, Barry Manilow, Madonna, and Jon Bon Jovi.

Wish I had her now: my first car, a hand-me-down 1962 Buick Skylark.

The guidance department folks, a disinterested bunch, agree I'm "pre-dental." I sign up for whatever chemistry, zoology, and math classes are required of freshmen. I coasted through high school, barely cracking a book unless for a test. A few weeks back, I was at the Woodstock festival surrounded by 250,000 freaks; the vibe was peace, love, and music. Now, I might have arrived on an alien planet. The library looms every night, grim and foreboding. The dorm is bare bones, a cinder-block structure divided into monkish cells furnished with metal frame beds and desks. At home, my mom furnished my room like Napoleon's retreat.

There, still working on his summer school math homework, sits my roommate, Andrew Keane Gwinn Scrivner III from Cockeysville; his country accent as memorable as his blueblood name. Andrew, who is a hairbreadth away from an academic meltdown, has adorned our room with photos of his blue ribbon-winning hog—whose name I can't recall—from the Timonium State Fair. It's clear I'm not going to be hanging out here.

It began with a toss of a Frisbee: Bobby and Larry Solomon, University of Maryland, 1973.

I take the elevator down from the seventh floor and head over to the mall. The rolling green space at the heart of the university cheers me up and the weather is beautiful. Students in jeans and shorts are running around laughing, flirting, joking, reading, a few tossing Frisbees. Someone is playing a guitar. Then it hits me: There's no one to tell me what to do except me!

I'm walking around amazed when a Frisbee skitters up to me, obviously gotten away from someone. Without a thought, I pick it up and fling it back. A curly haired guy grabs it and flings it right back at me. I send it back a little harder. So does he. It becomes one of those back-and-forth flinging matches, up to the point where we both start laughing. The guy comes up to me.

"I'm Larry Solomon," he says extending his hand. "I'm from Baltimore. I'm running for freshmen legislature."

"Okay."

And with the flick of a Frisbee, a star-crossed friendship that remains part of my life 50 years later is born.

"Who are you rooming with?" Larry asks that first afternoon.

"I got hooked up with this guy. We don't have a damn thing in common."

"I'm going to pledge a Jewish fraternity to get out of the dorms. You Jewish?"

"Why?"

"They have the best files."

He's talking about the legacy filing systems kept up by the Greek houses—years of recommendations and warnings about professors, old quizzes, papers, and tests, sometimes even final exams that many instructors can't be bothered to update.

"Sounds like a plan."

Next thing you know, we're Alpha Epsilon Pi pledges enduring the usual Hell Night scavenger hunt. In our case, collecting a pair of purple panties from a hooker on 14th and V Street in D.C., getting stripper Blaze Starr's autograph at the Gayety or the 2 O'Clock Club on The Block (East Baltimore Street), raiding the university president's backyard, and making off with gigantic, straw-filled archery targets. Four of us pledges spend the small hours of the night at Larry's mom's apartment playing poker. The next morning, his mom Rosalie cooks us breakfast. She's easygoing, open, and "with it." She'll become my security blanket when I'm feeling lonely or bummed out.

When my parents visit, Rosalie is the person I want them to meet. Some of Larry's Baltimore relatives are bookies, gamblers, and shady characters hanging out in pool halls and handicapping the ponies at Pimlico. I'm drawn to all this like metal to a magnet. My family, with its quirks and idiosyncrasies, secret histories and quiet frustrations, is what passes for normal in America. Rosalie and I will stay connected for the rest of her life.

Around this time, Carlson Woods Carter, a blonde, blue-eyed Tri Delt, the prettiest of the pretty in the sorority world, approaches me and strikes up a conversation. Carlson asks if I'll tutor her. She has three names and she says she's impressed with an answer I gave in English class?

How can I not agree?

Minister of Marriage: Bobby officiates at the wedding of Larry's daughter, Danielle Solomon and Sam Turner in Loveland, Colorado, August 31, 2013.

"You're gonna tutor Carlson Woods Carter?" Larry is astonished. "I can't believe it!"

"She's okay."

"The absolute cream of the crop!"

Carlson begins showing up at the fraternity house twice a week. We work together on essays and reports. Soon enough, we're goofing around, giggling around, fooling around. Unfortunately, Fraternity Row is horseshoe-shaped and Kappa Alpha sits directly across from AEPi. Therein lies the rub: A KA jock, claiming to be Carlson's boyfriend, spots her coming out of my frat house. To give you a sense of this place in 1969—after Woodstock and the moon landing—there's a KA tradition that once a year the frat boys gallop horses across the campus. Carlson's alleged beau, a handsome blond numbnut, rides a white stallion. (Over at AEPi, a horse is a thing you bet on.) Adonis corners me and basically tells me that if I want to live, I'd best keep my hands off Carlson. He's six foot three. I'm five foot eight. It's like Mutt and Jeff, only I'm not even Mutt.

No lasting human connection is ever as simple, as easy, as uncomplicated, or as painless as it first seems. Larry is from Pikesville, a mostly working-class neighborhood in Baltimore, the city Americans encounter 20 years later in *The Wire*: a once-thriving port plagued by poverty, drugs, violence, cynicism, and every kind of corruption. The only child of divorced parents, Larry is the guy who makes it out of the neighborhood, but carries the aspirations and expectations of his family and peers, a heavy burden. Like me, and everyone else on campus, Larry is trying to figure out who he is. Unlike me, he consciously plays different roles to different people—the cool guy, the ambitious guy, the stoner, the student government leader, the ladies' man. He's precocious and street smart, but basically out there on his own because Rosalie is more pal than parent. His father, a gambler who decides to reform by becoming an Orthodox Jew, is not a part of his life. His Italian grandfather, a tailor, makes him custom sharkskin suits with flaring bell-bottoms. Larry's style—many students are wearing madras pants—is more James Brown than Smothers Brothers.

Three for the road: Bobby, Elisa, and Larry Solomon. Rock Creek Park, Silver Springs, Maryland, 1978.

Over time, I come to realize that behind his confident façade, Larry struggles, but to my 18-year-old self, he's pure fun, always pedal to the metal—no one is gonna take his T-Bird away. Larry is also ambitious, seemingly a man with a plan. At one point he tells me he is going to own Udels, the best-known photography studio in the city. Like most of our peers, he's a stoner; unlike most of us, he pushes things to the limit and often beyond.

"I want you to be my campaign manager," Larry says that first day.

"Are you serious?"

"Yes."

On the plus side, Larry is a man of his word. He's color-blind. He sees things that don't sit right with him and wants to be a force for change. That speaks to me, so I agree. He also knows his way around, knows Baltimore and Washington, knows how to get to the track, and knows where the best parties are. At that point, Roy Coopersmith, a veteran student government leader, also from Baltimore, takes us to the AEPi basement "war room" where we make "Vote for Solomon for Freshmen Legislature" posters on tagboard. Larry adds a high school resume as long as my arm—senior class representative, banquet committee, varsity golf, lacrosse, etc. and a 10-point agenda covering everything from enhanced pre-registration to combating "institutional racism." Where the hell this comes from I have no idea.

It's doubtful that a high-minded appeal will win him the election. Most male students are interested in beer and wet T-shirts. And College Park, Maryland, is still a conservative place. Like most Baltimoreans on campus, Larry has an inner-city edge that small-town students find off-putting, particularly farmers and frat boys. His budding Afro doesn't help his cause either. But, of course, Larry has a plan. In a world before Google and the Internet, he's mined the data: He knows there are twice as many freshmen girls as guys; that the women live in two 9-story dorms—Centreville and Arundel Hall; and that only freshmen can vote for freshmen candidates.

"Let's canvass the women's dorms."

We're not allowed in at night, but during the day we go floor-to-floor, knocking on each door all the way up and all the way down. We introduce ourselves and explain that Larry Solomon is a good man, but he can't win unless "you girls win it for him." We also ask the women not to vote until half an hour before the polls close—so there's no counterresponse from Larry's opponents—then we want them all to parade in. Sure enough, this happens: a big migration of girls funneling out of the two dorms, our frat guys marching behind, all heading to the polls. The girls love it. I love it. It's so cool.

Larry wins in a landslide.

That election is the high point of Larry's college career. By sophomore year, he is in an academic nosedive and trying to avoid corkscrewing into the ground. That very first day, I saw so much potential in Larry—how smart, sensitive, and charismatic he was and what an astonishing memory he had, but then I notice other things, unsettling things. Whether it's drinking or smoking pot, Larry is always out front, getting blasted. He leads the charge at the local pizza parlor where the nightly "beer race" is a big event. He's the guy always ready to cross, sniff, or snort the line, any line. The guy drawn to danger. One day, he shows up on a motorcycle. My whole life it's been planted in my head that riding a motorcycle will get you killed.

Good looks and charisma: Nadine and Larry Solomon.

"Bobby, don't bum me out."

Next thing I know, I'm on the back of his motorcycle, grinning. We're roaring up I-95 to Pimlico. Like half of Baltimore, Larry loves thoroughbred racing, the sport of kings, a confounding, adrenaline-fueled passion I happily embrace. In 1972, Larry, Brian "Hardy" Hardwick, Kenny "Kozo" Kondritzer, and I break out of campus and attend all three legs of the Triple Crown. It's one of the highlight buddy adventures of my life.

Larry is all fun, all the time; high school all over again. In my car or in his mother's car, Larry stomps the gas at every light trying to burn rubber. I sit there, knees up on the dash, waiting for the crash. Socially, he's a butterfly, all over the place. He falls for this beautiful, hard-looking girl named Nadine because she's wild, like a tomboy. He teaches himself to swivel his feet like James Brown. Wearing his bell-bottom suit, Larry shows up at frat parties with Nadine and they strut their stuff in the line dances. Everyone laughs and cheers them on. He basks in the attention.

Now, I realize there were things going on in his life, things Larry knew I wouldn't be a part of. He rents a house with some other guys. Nadine moves in with him. The two will marry, but it doesn't last. At a party there, I see this whole other world—slurring stoners handing out Tuinals, Seconals, Quaaludes, with worse stuff going on in the bathrooms. Larry's in the kitchen, not a care in the world, cooking veal francese! He's battering, got the whole counter covered with flour, and he's pounding away. Flour is flying everywhere. He makes this great meal for all these strangers. Afterward, the house looks like it's been hit by a tornado. Nadine, no doubt, is left to clean it all up.

Nadine, Larry, and Bobby. Here's to the good times!

I can see where things are heading, but our friendship is so important—to both of us—that I stay silent. Neither Larry nor I have brothers. His family is dysfunctional. My parents, for lack of a better term, are self-involved. My sister is sweet but we don't have a deep relationship. My friends become my family. I turn to them when I'm troubled.

Larry turns to heroin. None of it happens overnight. During our junior year, I sense we've been drifting apart—two young men full of ourselves, pursuing different courses of study, engaging with new people and in new relationships. After graduation, when I move to Atlanta for law school, Larry and I continue to have the deep, soul-searching conversations that are the foundation of our friendship—politics, parents, career aspirations, his troubled relationship with Nadine, the daunting infertility problems Elisa and I are facing. One topic that never comes up is his escalating drug use. In our late twenties, Larry, Nadine, Elisa, and I travel to Valentine's Resort and Marina on Eleuthera, a secluded pink-and-turquoise jewel in the Bahamas. Nadine keeps hinting that her marriage is blowing apart, but you'd never guess it with Larry.

At one point, he spots two kids riding horses so skinny their spines stick out.

"Come on!" he shouts. "Let's go get 'em!"

"Larry," I say, "they're riding bareback."

Money changes hands. Reluctantly, the kids turn over the horses. Next thing I know, we're riding down the beach. I'm hanging on for dear life. Larry is galloping, whipping the horses, flying over the sand. As if by some prearranged signal, both nags stop short, and we go flying over their necks into a pile of sand. We're bruised and covered in sand laughing hysterically—until the horses run off. It takes an hour to round them up.

While still in school, Larry takes a part-time job at Udel Brothers on Charles Street, the most prestigious photo studio in the city, the place where the mayor and the governor have their portraits made. He has a genuine feel for photography and, of course, a street hustler's charm. Soon, he's gone from apprentice to George Udel's protégé. At graduation, Larry invites me to lunch at the 100-year-old Harvey House close by the studio, an eclectic place favored by both rowdy Colts fans and Baltimore Symphony aficionados, famous for its onion soup, crab cakes, and prime rib.

"I'm going to own Udel Brothers," Larry announces confidently.

"Great! Will you shoot my wedding?" (At this point, I don't have a girlfriend.)

"Be honored."

There's a black-and-white photograph of us taken that day. I've looked at it recently. My eyes are clear, bright, and eager; in Larry's eyes, a creeping desperation that somehow I'd missed.

In 1973, I move to Atlanta to attend John Marshall Law School. I meet Elisa Zwecker and enter into the relationship that is still vibrant today. Time passes, as it inevitably does. What word I have from Larry is that he's doing very well. He's bought the Udel Brothers studio, a house, and is earning upwards of $100,000. In fact, he's doing a hell of a lot better than I am. Rosalie is overseeing the business for him. Unknown to me, Larry is also haunting another Baltimore, not the city he loves so much and knows so well with its funky restaurants and zany characters, but the decaying warehouses of the Inner Harbor, the open-air drug markets of Sandtown, the rabbit warren of mean streets radiating off Old Town Mall.

Surf's up in the Eleutheras: Hangin' with Larry was unbridled fun.

A day comes when I take the call. Rosalie is panicked and in tears, telling me Larry's missing appointments, screwing up photo shoots, bills are piling up, the books are a mess. Money is flying out the door. Larry has always been a prince who can do no wrong, so Rosalie has been in denial, making the excuses addicts' loved ones always make and only fool themselves. Larry has left hypodermic needles, ties, cotton balls, spoons, blood on the toilet seat—his "works"—in a bathroom his own mother uses.

"Bobby, I don't know what I'm going to do!"

"I'll be on the next plane."

Honestly, the years that follow are blurred except for the pain everyone endures. I remember calling our friend and AEPi brother Brian Hardwick who's living near Baltimore. Together, we track down and confront Larry—he's totally out of control—and force him into the first of many rehabs. I now realize these places are mostly useless, be they high-end, low-end, locked-down psych wards, or blissful meditative resorts in the southwestern desert. The odds that a hard-core heroin addict will "recover" and become a productive member of society are miniscule. Some have overblown names like "Male Crisis Stabilization" programs, many overpromise everything, and all are seemingly designed to extract the maximum amount of money before their desperate clients' assets and insurance coverage run out. Larry slips in and out of sobriety, sometimes for weeks, even a few years, but I come to appreciate opiate addiction is not a habit, but a disease as relentless and deadly as pancreatic cancer.

A clever guy, Larry, learns the ropes, says the right things to Dr. Wormser, his German shrink and in the "rooms," but he never, ever breaks free. In a 12-step meeting, he meets Jodie, a struggling alcoholic, never a good idea. They marry—that union lasts barely two years—but Jodie presents Larry with a baby girl, Danielle, a daughter so extraordinary that all the best of Larry lives in her. The proud grandmother, Rosalie, does all she can to support them. Not enough, never enough. Larry starts another photography business; this one more modest, focused on graduation and prom pictures, but he's running on empty. No money, no car, no insurance, no options.

Larry and Nadine egg me on to eat a raw conch: "It'll put lead in your pencil, man!"

This time the call comes at 2:30 a.m. Elisa and I are in bed, struggling through our fourth or fifth in vitro attempt to get pregnant. "I'm suicidal," he tells me. "Devils are calling to him" like sirens in the harbor. I talk him down. Elisa and I invite him to Atlanta to live with us, a choice that's easy to question if you don't have to make it. My relationship with Larry is literally part of me, as complex and intricate as the neural pathways in my brain. That it's broken compels me to try to fix it. Larry flies down and prepares to go into rehab yet again. The counselors at Anchor Hospital have some hard talks with Elisa and me, "You need to let him hit rock bottom."

Before checking in, Larry stops by my law office in the Equitable Building, high above the city. We're sprouting our feathers, putting on a good show for our prospective clients. Larry looks around, the city stretching out below. He's going into a month-long, brutal, no-frills course of treatment.

"I've gotta cut you off," I tell him.

It's the hardest thing I've ever said. "I'm not going to enable you. Elisa is not going to enable you. You've got to do this thing on your own. We'll be there at the end." I still see him walking down the hallway to the elevator. I want to run to him, but I don't.

Larry lives with us until he's ready to make it on his own. It's one of those moments when I realize the importance of family. Elisa's father finds him a small apartment; we buy him a ratty powder-blue Mustang, the cheapest car on the lot. He gets a very modest job, making photos at the mall. I know things will never be the same between us, the fun and joking and all that stuff, but in some ways, Larry and I grow even closer. Nothing is hidden. Larry, stripped naked, is accepted unconditionally. The same way he accepted me and all our friends, unconditionally. He's finely attuned to Elisa's fragile emotional state. He remembers the tiniest details—the first time they met; things she'd said, done, or worn; and the fun we'd had together back in the day. Elisa will cherish these intense conversations when fate or destiny disorders our lives.

You couldn't see a cloud in the sky: Bobby and Monte, Valentine's Yacht Club in Harbor Island, Eleuthera.

In Baltimore, Larry undergoes a long-neglected knee replacement surgery. He's not mobile enough to work efficiently as a photographer. He tells me he's uneasy about taking any drugs, even what he needs to ease his pain. The surgery goes forward without complication. His doctors keep him in recovery an extra day or so. They know he's got a bad history. This time when the call comes, I'm neither surprised nor shocked. Life is going to unfold the way life is going to unfold. Larry dies of heart failure in the hospital.

He's 48 years old.

I am the person I am—the boy who picked up the Frisbee a half-century ago—to whom love, friendship, and loyalty remain the greatest virtues. I stay in touch with Rosalie for the rest of her life. She has more than her share of challenges, but also joy—she lives to see Danielle, Larry's daughter, blossom into a brilliant, loving, and sensitive young woman. "Uncle" Bobby and "Aunt" Elisa are there when Danielle is in preschool, when she graduates college, when she lands a job as Wolf Blitzer's producer on CNN, and when she converts her Atlanta condo into a hospice for the fading Rosalie.

Danielle and her fiancé, Sam Turner, a smart, attentive, compassionate man, invite me to officiate at their wedding in Colorado, a sunlit place far from the grim streets of Baltimore. I stand before the gathered assembly of strangers, seeing them through a jeweler's eye—Larry's eye—honored and bereft, as a mosaic of images, memories, songs, ineffable loss, and joy—the very elements of Larry's being—sparkle in the sunlit mountain air.

BOBBY EZOR | ORDINARY LIFE IS EXTRAORDINARY

Chapter 7

A Box of Homemade Rugelach

Some months have passed since I passed the Georgia Bar Exam. I'm working part-time for one of my law school professors, Jim Pilcher, but I haven't tried my first case. I'm living on Atlanta's West Side in a very modest apartment complex near the Water Works, also home to the inimitable Irwin Deutsch. Most afternoons, when I arrive home, two fishbelly-white legs are sticking out from under a broken-down junker.

"How you doing Lee?" I'd say, reaching for my keys.

This day, Lee, a big, sweaty guy covered in grease, slides out from under the car.

"Not so good," he says softly. "You a lawyer now?"

"Yup."

"Can I talk to you a minute?"

Lee is my neighbor. Overweight with sad-sack eyes, thick glasses with oversize black frames. At the time, hipsters in Hotlanta sport bouffant hair and satin Bee Gee jackets. Lee is your average Joe. He has a McJob, is trying to save money, probably counts the times he's been with a woman on one hand. Turns out I'm wrong about that last one.

"What's going on?"

"This woman filed for a divorce," he says. He's talking about his wife. "I don't know what to do. I don't have the money to pay a high-class lawyer. (Thanks Lee!)"

I don't know anything about divorce other than what I've read in a textbook, but I could see Lee getting sucked in. Maybe he went to some predatory singles bar like Atlanta's notorious Johnny's Hideaway and was taken for a ride. A moment later, the story is pouring out of him like he's the Ancient Mariner. The "woman" who has filed for divorce is literally a poor man's Candace Mossler.

If you don't recall the tabloid potboiler, Candace was allegedly involved in one of the more scandalous murders of the last half-century—and got away with it. In June 1964, Georgia-born Candace (nee: Weatherby), the estranged blonde bombshell wife of an octogenarian Texas millionaire named Jacques Mossler, was shocked to learn that Jacques' bludgeoned and bloody corpse—he'd been stabbed 39 times—was found in her Key Biscayne, Florida, apartment.

To her, I walked on water: Mom and me, 1978.

Candace had a solid alibi—she was at an area hospital with two of her children after suffering a debilitating migraine, but her alleged lover (and nephew) Melvin Powers left a trail of evidence at the crime scene. A year later, after much legal wrangling, Powers was extradited to Miami where he and Candace were charged with first-degree murder. The trial was so lurid—think O.J. Simpson and Amanda Knox rolled into one—the presiding judge barred minors from the courtroom and one Miami newspaper literally printed "Extras" on pink newsprint.

Thanks to some seemingly miraculous legal defense maneuvering and courtroom histrionics of lawyers Percy Foreman, Clyde Woody, and Marian Rosen not a single defense witness was called to testify. Candace and Melvin were acquitted. The lovers left the courtroom, strolled past a horde of reporters, and drove off into the sunset in a gold Cadillac.

Lee tells me Eve, his estranged wife, is Candace Mossler's kid sister. "She's done this eight or nine times," he moans. "Now she's hooked me and is going to take me for whatever I have."

I roll my eyes. "How do you know?" I demand.

"I've got some leads," he says. "But I don't have the wherewithal to do it."

While working with Jim Pilcher, I occasionally have to hire a private eye. I contact the investigator and pass him a few of Lee's leads. Sure enough, it's the truth. The investigator shows me a series of divorce decrees from around the Southeast, all granted to my client's wife. Her name is slightly different on the decrees, but the signature is undoubtedly the same. Apparently, she marries these guys for a short period of time and then files for divorce. Her modus operandi: "Give me $50,000 and I'll go away." Lee is about to get clobbered, probably another in an unending series of life's indignities. I feel for him. I take the case and agree to a fee of around $300. I gather the evidence and prep for my first trial. This is a real Perry Mason moment for me.

Of course, I call my mom in Paterson. "Mom, I'm having my first solo trial."

"Who's the judge?"

"Judge Fryer is presiding."

"This, I gotta see!"

She flies down here, one of the few times in her life she travels without my father. Of course, she does not come unprepared.

One stylish lady: Mom at our rehearsal dinner.

Judge Joel Fryer is the "Jewish" Superior Court judge, the first Jewish jurist to reach the trial court level in Georgia, an accomplishment apparently so extraordinary he's listed in *Who's Who in America*. Fryer is well respected in both the legal and Jewish communities. In fact, I see people crowding around him on the high holidays at Ahavath Achim Synagogue, eager to shake his hand. The judge has bushy eyebrows and horn-rimmed glasses, reminding me of Groucho Marx. So here I am, my first case with the Jewish superior court judge who knows everybody in my synagogue and my community. I'm a little edgy.

During one of the preliminary hearings, Judge Fryer looks up over his glasses—his eyebrows lift like flapping window shades. "Mr. Ezor," he says, "how many hours have you been in the law library this week?"

He wants to make sure I'm not screwing around. "Well, I was there only yesterday," I squeak.

"Only yesterday?" he says. "Or the last time was yesterday?"

The day of the trial finally arrives. I'm in my three-piece suit. Lee is sitting next to me, a hangdog look on his face. The divorce decrees are in front of me like hole cards in a poker game. Eve is sitting at the other table with her attorney, a big, buxom woman engulfed in a cloud of perfume and hairspray. My mother is two rows back. Next to her is a little white box with a string tied around it.

The case proceeds. On cross-examination, I ask Eve, "Have you ever been divorced before?"

"No," she responds instantly.

"I remind you that you that you are under oath," I say, doing my best Perry Mason imitation. "Before you answer, please think about it."

And she could bake some mean Rugelach: Mom at our wedding, 1979.

"No," she repeats. "I've not been married before."

"Really?"

One by one, I take out the divorce decrees. "Is this your signature?"

"No. It looks like my signature, but that's not my name."

I take the next one out, then the next, and the next. "Is this...Is this...this?"

Finally, a bewildered Judge Fryer orders me to bring these decrees up to him. He looks at them and the courtroom falls silent.

"Psst! Psst!" It's Mom, her Jersey-Yiddish accent unmistakable. "Psst!"

Judge Fryer looks up and frowns. "Mr. Ezor, will you approach the bench?" This is not a question. "What's going on here?" he demands.

"Well, your Honor. This is going to sound ridiculous, but my mother wanted to see me try my first trial. She brought a box of homemade rugelach. They're for you."

"Tell your mother to behave. She'll have to wait until we're done with our proceeding."

I walk back to the bar. "Mom, please sit back. You're getting me in hot water."

"But I want to give the judge…"

"You can't do it that way, Mom!" There it was, my whole life reduced to a pastry box with a string around it.

I go through the rest of the decrees. Judge Fryer finally registers what's going on. Scowling, he orders Eve taken into custody for perjury. The bailiff comes up and takes her away. Next, Fryer dismisses the divorce action against Lee. The marriage will be annulled at a later date. We're walking out of the courtroom. I can finally breathe.

Mom at home in her kitchen in Paterson.

"Mr. Ezor," Judge Fryer says.

I stiffen. "Your Honor?"

"I'll have those rugelach now."

"Ah yes, Your Honor. This is my mother, Estelle Ezor."

"How are you, Mrs. Ezor?" the judge makes some small talk, then adds, "I love homemade rugelach. One of my favorites!"

We all have a laugh over that.

BOBBY EZOR | ORDINARY LIFE IS EXTRAORDINARY

Chapter 8

Zwecker Rhymes with Checker!

79

Tying the knot on October 21, 1979: Elisa's brother Mark. Dad exalted by Lester "Mr. Wonderful" Benowitz and my pal/photographer Larry Solomon. Grandma Sadie and Grandma Bedie share the joy.

Zwecker

is the last name on the last page of the Atlanta phone book. I discover this fact while running a storefront law office in the Stewart-Lakewood shopping center in south Atlanta. Along with my neighbors—bakery, barber shop, bank, and discount furniture store—I'm hoping for my first customer of the day. Across the mall, Clark's Gas ("miles of smiles") and Funtown Amusement Center with its fake tombstones ("Here lies Mr. Meek. He forgot to turn the other cheek!") bake in the southern heat.

I'm a third-year law school student, prepping for the bar exam. For company, I have Jesse, my 130-pound Saint Bernard snoozing outside the door, and two gigantic law review books on my desk, so when Bell South drops off the new directories that's exciting. This is the world before the Internet, social media, and smartphones.

I've been clerking for one of my professors, James B. Pilcher Esq., who decides I'm competent enough to run his firm's satellite office. I do everything: answer phones, sign up clients, draw up contracts, handle preliminary work for divorce actions and torts, even work on some minor criminal defense cases. I get maybe two or three people a day, about the same as the furniture guy a few doors down. Most folks are more interested in Jesse than my legal acuity, but if nothing else, I'm eager, personable, and willing to work hard. I make a point of meeting all the proprietors in the strip mall and before long I'm essentially Stewart-Lakewood's go-to lawyer.

Looking back, I'm pretty sure I represented everyone in that mall. I had this little family thing going on. Jim Pilcher saw me as a rainmaker. Meanwhile, around the corner, not far from the federal penitentiary on McDonough Street, sits Harold's Barbeque, a smoke-stained and aroma-filled Atlanta landmark. Harold's is a hangout for everyone—from law enforcement and local politicians to the judges, prosecutors, bailiffs, and secretaries, trial lawyers, and public defenders—the whole constellation

Deep in a dream of you: Elisa and me.

that comprises the judicial universe. I'm savvy enough to introduce myself to many of these people, and they come to recognize my face, a connection, by the way, that will later help me tremendously in my practice.

I've been breezing through John Marshall Law School, carefree as a clam until I meet some frazzled students from Emory University's School of Law. It hits me—like an icy tingle in my spine—that I have to dramatically up my game if I'm going to pass the bar. I begin to study with the Emory guys, making sure I have the right textbooks and do all the right things. Still, the pressure is really freaking people out—some students have job offers contingent on passing the exam.

So I decide to host a pre-bar exam "Break the Ice" party one Saturday night. Seventy people show up. I'm walking through my crowded house, meeting and greeting, when I overhear some women chattering away in an alcove. One says, "Elisa Zwecker is back in town, we ought to get together." Another says, "Zwecker rhymes with checker!" That grabs my attention. I stop, chat—one of them is a woman named Carol Goodman—and move on. This Elisa sounds like a cool kid. For the next few hours I mimic, "Zwecker rhymes with checker."

Back at the Stewart-Lakewood office, I open the Atlanta phone book and the very last listing is Jack Zwecker. I call and a woman answers in what I'll call a southern Jewish drawl, not molasses, but a hint of Yiddish. I've just met my future mother-in-law.

"Hello."

A couple of castaways.

"This is Bobby Ezor, a friend of Elisa's," a fib, but well-intentioned.

"Oh!" she says, sounding pleased."

Sophie Zwecker gives me her daughter's home number and work number, and tells me where she lives and the bank branch where she's employed. She doesn't know who I am or the first thing about me. I might be the Boston Strangler for all she knows, but in Atlanta, this is apparently acceptable behavior.

It's May 1976, six weeks before the bar exam.

I call Fulton National Bank's Howell Mill Road branch and ask to speak to "Ms. Elisa Zwecker." After a few minutes, she comes on the line and I blurt, "Hi, I'm Bobby Ezor. Carol Goodman mentioned your name at my party. She said 'Zwecker rhymes with checker!' You sounded interesting and I thought you might want to have dinner with me."

Clowning with one of my favorite people, my son Zack.

Silence. Then, after a long pause: "How did you get my number?"

I have a ready answer. "Your mother gave it to me."

"What?"

"She gave me all your information."

"What?"

"I'm perfectly safe. I have a Saint Bernard."

At 24, I'm at a point where I'm looking for a meaningful relationship.

"This sounds a little weird, but okay. When do you want to get together?"

"Six weeks."

"Six weeks! That's very weird."

"I'm studying for the bar exam and can't get distracted, but I really wanted to touch base."

"Yeah, sure."

The next day, I call the bank again. She comes to the phone. After the second or third time, Elisa says, "I can't take these personal calls at work. You can call me at home in the evening."

"Really?"

That month we must talk 30 to 40 times. We become friends—not so different from the way my parents, Sheldon and Estelle, and millions of the Greatest Generation used V-Mail to get to know each other during World War II. I don't know what she looks like, her politics, how she dresses, or what perfume she wears, but I feel her heart, sense her intelligence, maybe even glimpse her soul. At a distance, strange as it may sound, we get to know one another openly and honestly. We discover we like each other, an attraction that grows into the bond that will hold us together for the rest of our lives.

Daughter Dani and her Dad play Eloise at The Plaza Hotel, Manhattan.

I'd be less than honest—not the real Bobby Ezor—if I didn't say the girls I'd met at my party were good-looking, so I figured good-looking girls hang out with good-looking girls. I never really thought about it. Friendship was what was most important, the same way I knew Danny Lawrence, Scott Kessler, Barry Spector, Larry Urbach, Larry Solomon, Brian Hardwick, and I were going to be friends no matter what happened. I don't let go of things easily.

I pass the bar exam.

Elisa and I finally meet. Not long after, we commit to building the relationship on display on every page of this book, if not in detail, then in spirit. We're yin and yang, seemingly opposite forces that complement each other: When I get crazy, Elisa, cooler, quieter, and more still, makes sure it's not too crazy. When she's stuck in the mud, my nonstop energy, motion, and loudness guarantee she doesn't miss the fun. On her birthday, I surprise her with a mystery trip—to the Borscht Belt, the legendary "Jewish Alps" where I'd had some great times with my parents. I've rounded up three or four couples; they're already onboard our Delta flight when we show up. Elisa, Georgia-born, doesn't know what the Catskills are; they might as well be the Pyramids. Limousines are waiting at LaGuardia. And we're off! We spend the weekend at the Concord, faded but still clinging to the old traditions, one of which is over-the-top theatrics on both sides of the stage: You schmear the maître d', theater managers, cocktail waitresses, waiters, busboys. And they, in turn, make you feel you are the one and only customer.

When menus appear, I schmear our waiter.

"What are you doing?" Elisa asks puzzled.

Poof! The menus disappear. They bring us everything.

That part hasn't changed.

The Joys of Parenting: Bobby at two. Dad and Dani ready for the square dance. Elisa and Zack Eskimo kiss.

Zack teaching me to blow bubbles. Dad and Dani Eskimo kiss. Our second Saint Bernard Mickey (named after you-know-who). Elisa and Bobby at Zack's first birthday party ("Young At Heart" theme). Our first Saint Bernard Jessica (named after Allman Brothers instrumental).

Zack with our first grandchild Sammy. Bobby and Elisa with our lifelong keeper of the house Carrie Jane Sutton. My favorite backpack on Cumberland Island, 1989.

Cupid asked and she said "Yes." Bobby and Lisa ride Testudo. Bobby at Zack's Duke Law graduation. Dani and Lichtenstein.

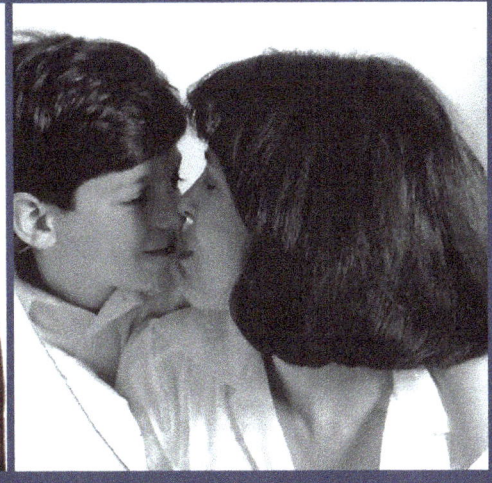

BOBBY EZOR | ORDINARY LIFE IS EXTRAORDINARY

Chapter 9

The accidental wrong turn is what makes a trip worthwhile.

4073
Cost of War

Chip

Simone and I are close friends but we've never seen each other's hometowns. We entertain ourselves with hometown stories—things you carry in your head—of adolescent mischief, joy, pain, sex, music, friends, teachers, parents, and the peculiar characters who immigrated into our respective neighborhoods. I'm a sports guy, a jock, a chronicler of batting averages and home runs. Chip, an artsy type, uses his camera to see and shield himself from the world. He's from working-class Worcester, Massachusetts. I grew up comfortably in Paterson, New Jersey, a city in steep decline at the time. One summer morning, Chip is talking, painting images of his childhood. I feel I'm almost there with him, but with me "almost" is never enough.

"I want to see it," I say. "Let's do a road trip. We'll stop in Paterson on the way."

It's roughly 900 miles via I-81 from Atlanta to Paterson, and another 300 to Worcester, our turnaround. This is 2003, so we're navigating via gas station maps and the primitive GPS unit in my Acura. Make one unprogrammed turn and it corrects over and over until you want to scream. Giddy as schoolboys on the first day of summer vacation, we head north, part of that great American love affair with roads, cars, travel, speed, wide-open spaces. Like Jack Kerouac and Neal Cassady, only with wives and careers and mortgages. I'm not a voracious reader, but I love good stories. Words—dialogues, songs, tales, remembrances—intoxicate me. I listen so intently that strangers take me for a therapist.

Chip's hometown tales are peopled by mobsters, bookies, schemers, and corrupt priests. His aunties, devout Catholics, swear like dockworkers; his mother struggles to protect her sensitive, artistic boy from his father's unpredictable rages. On Chip's first date—he tells me—he wants to borrow the family car, hardly a bizarre request.

When he asks, his dad literally knocks him across the room. This is not my world. I was captain of my high school's tennis team. I was an editor of the newspaper. My dad ran an encyclopedia company. My mom's biggest challenge seemed to be selecting the right decorator to redo our living room, though this would change.

My good friend Chippa: Robert "Chip" Simone, photographer.

As the hours tick by, Chip's sonorous voice merges with the hum of tires and the engine's muffled throb. A night in a cheap motel and day one merges into day two. That second afternoon, we're so deep in conversation that I fail to heed the GPS's insistent "Recalculating...Recalculating...Recalculating."

"Shit! We're way off course!"

Actually, we're hundreds of miles off course, in Parkersburg, West Virginia. That's the Ohio River up ahead, not the Hudson. Looking for a turnaround to head back east, I find myself in a tangle of country roads.

"Wow, did you see that!" Chip exclaims.

"What?"

"The setting sun reflecting on a hillside. I swear it looked like a UFO."

"Let's go find it, whatever it is."

All thoughts of maps and time and directions fly out the window. That's the point. Most people would say, "It's late. It's getting get dark. We're already lost. Let's get back on the road." We start back to where Chip thinks he saw this glow. He can't find it and we go back and forth, making U-turns trying to matrix the area.

"I see it!" he finally shouts.

We come off this little road and down a hill. There's an old-fashioned service station with a couple gas pumps and these ol' boys in coveralls sitting outside, almost a stereotype. I pull over and get out.

"We saw something strange out there," I begin, trying to find the right words, "like a hillside of light?" They look at each other.

"Y'all talking 'bout so and so's graveyard?" one offers.

"Graveyard?" This is not what I expect.

They point us in the right direction. Ten minutes later, we bump our way onto the property. Big dogs, barking and snarling, rush to greet us.

The Parkway Diner in Worcester, Massachusetts. Chip's hometown!

"You're good with dogs," I smile at Chip.

"Screw you!" he gets out and disappears, the dogs at his heels.

It's true. Chip, who's owned a string of white German Shepherds, is a pre-Cesar Millan dog whisperer. After a few minutes, he returns without the pack and I get out of the car. Above me, on the slopes of a verdant hillside, must be 2,000 white crosses glittering in the fading sunlight. I spot a wheelbarrow piled with more crosses and then a man on his knees planting individual crosses in the ground.

We approach and start a conversation, one of the great joys of the road. It turns out the man is a Vietnam vet, a fierce critic of the 2003 invasion of Iraq which, as I write these words, has led to approximately 5,000 American casualties and 17 years of chaos and bloodshed, the rise of Al Qaeda in Iraq, Isis, and Bashar al-Assad's endless massacres in Syria.

Chip grabs his Nikon and begins photographing the hillside. The man on the hill, whose name is lost to time, views his art installation—though he would not be familiar with the term—as a symbol for the ongoing tragedy. Each week, together with a group of college students, he scans the newspapers and gets a casualty count. They put the crosses in the ground and hold a brief memorial service. On this forgotten hillside, the impact is devastating, a miniature of the heartbreaking rows, "the gardens of stone," in Arlington National Cemetery.

In the Berkshires: Chip Simone, Elisa, and Kathy Egan (Chip's wife), overlooking the Stockbridge Bowl.

I'm heading back to the car when the man's wife appears. She wears a simple dress and apron, almost a stereotype of the farmers' wives you see in children's books. We exchange pleasantries. I'm curious, and she doesn't get much company. In minutes, she's telling me about her life, her family, her community, and of course, the man on the hill. Vietnam was sweeping through America's rural communities like a scythe when they fell in love. After high school, he enlisted in the Marines—my teenage father did the same in WWII—and she dreaded each moment he was gone. A lifetime later she says it's happening again to a new generation of wives and mothers. A random encounter becomes a transformative moment. My openness is a blessing: A complete stranger becomes a kindred spirt and then a friend. Even as I know I will never see her again.

Somehow, I'd mentioned that I'd played the clarinet in my high school marching band. It turns out that Parkersburg, this flyspeck on a map, once boasted the most famous high school band in the world. The Big Red Marching Band played at the Kentucky Derby and performed for President Ronald Reagan and the Queen of Romania. The list of accolades and awards is endless. She pulls out some photo albums and shows me, year by year, faded pictures of Big Red in action. Her husband—the man on the hill—was a clarinet player, same as me. Delicately, she removes an instrument case from a bulging closet and opens it. I smile. When Big Red won a national championship—there were many—Woody Herman, the legendary swing clarinet player and one of my idols, presented him with this instrument. A powerful desire to hold it sweeps over me, a need, perhaps, to renew long-ago connections. She insists we stay for dinner.

A simple meal as I recall—meat, potatoes, and peas. But like the lonely memorial on the hill, it has stayed with me all these years.

The man on the hill: Parkersburg, West Virginia.

I've never had a friend like you
As passionate about life
So endlessly curious
Of such generous spirit
Shark that you are
Swimming always
Afraid to miss the next wonderful thing
By drowning in your sleep

Thanks for the great trip
Love always,
Chip
July 2002

I'm not in Kansas anymore! Chip Simone and I are driving east on Brooklyn's Belt Parkway headed to Sag Harbor when the sign beckons: "Coney Island!" All thoughts of the frou-frou Hamptons fly out the window. Next thing I know I'm strolling down Surf Avenue eating a Nathan's Famous and munching on a soft ice cream cone, known locally as a "Carvel." All the while drawn irresistibly toward the legendary "Cyclone." roller coaster.

BOBBY EZOR | ORDINARY LIFE IS EXTRAORDINARY

Chapter 10

He was as great as great could be.

Muhammad Ali and me

I'm  12 when Cassius Clay fights Sonny Liston in Miami Beach. America is pulling for Liston, the glowering convicted felon controlled by the Italian mob over the clean-cut, brash, gifted, and endlessly voluble Olympic champion. "Liston is gonna zip The Lip!" the seventh-grade boys in my class at P.S. 20 chortle. "Liston is gonna zip The Lip!" The prediction is trumpeted on TV, in the sporting press, in the tabloids, in every tavern, and on every street corner in the country. My classmate Danny Ginsburg and I know otherwise. We're pulling for "The Lip," a self-proclaimed poet—"floats like a butterfly, stings like a bee"—who will become the most famous man on earth.

My father, a Liston fan, takes me to the fight at the Teaneck Armory, no doubt looking to teach me a lesson in humility. Instead, the crowd goes berserk when Liston, soundly beaten, does not answer the bell for the seventh round. This is the first skirmish in a generational battle, one fought at kitchen tables and in living rooms all over the country—baby boomers versus the establishment, winner takes all. "Liston used to be a hoodlum," writes the editor of the *New Republic*. "Now he's our cop, the big Negro we pay to keep sassy Negroes in line."

At school, Danny Ginsburg and I strut like peacocks as Clay becomes the next great obsession of my life. After the second Liston fight, Cassius Clay converts to Islam, adopts the name Muhammad Ali, and seduces Howard Cosell, the sporting media, and the cocktail party intellectuals with his doggerel poetry (years before the first rapper), wit, and ebullience. During the buildup to the Vietnam War, Ali refuses induction into the military—"No Vietcong ever called me a nigger!"—he says, perfectly framing his conscientious objection. He's convicted, fined, and sentenced to five years in prison, his boxing license revoked. Things repeat themselves where Black lives are concerned. A half-century before, Jack Johnson the first Black heavyweight champion was reviled as an "uppity Negro." He was tried and convicted under the Mann Act for crossing a state line with a white woman. She happened to be his wife.

By 1970, the Zeitgeist has changed: Ali is now avatar, hero, global phenom, and a massive draw financially. His boxing license is reinstated, setting the stage for three epic battles with Joe Frazier. In 1971, at Madison Square Garden, Frazier survives a brutal, punishing encounter—the "Fight of the Century"—that leaves both men debilitated. In January 1974, Ali beats Frazier at Madison Square Garden by unanimous decision. (Both men are seemingly in decline: Frazier gets crushed by Olympic champion George Foreman in January 1973; that same year Ken Norton decisions Ali and breaks his jaw.)

Checking the ropes for Ali-Spinks II. Superdome, New Orleans, September 15, 1978.

In October 1975, I'm studying at John Marshall School of Law in Atlanta. Mark Rosenthal, one of my old Hebrew school classmates from Jersey, is in town on a management internship at Grady Hospital. When you fall in love—be it with the Yankees, the Grateful Dead, Sofia Loren, or Ali—you migrate toward other people who share your love. Nothing is pure coincidence. Hence, my unbreakable bond with the irascible Irwin Deutsch was grounded in our mutual love for Mickey Mantle. Through Mark, I meet Dr. Ernesto, a Filipino anesthesiologist who works at Grady. Ernesto knows his way around Manilla. He speaks perfect English. He's a big boxing fan. The most anticipated fight on the planet is on the horizon. The pieces are coming together: The third and final showdown between two of boxing's greatest heavyweights will be decided in the middle of the Pacific.

Of course, I'm in.

Ali versus Frazier at the Araneta Coliseum is the "Thrilla in Manila." Getting there involves a three-week 7,300-mile passage on a tramp steamer that may or may not include stowing away on a lifeboat lashed to the deck. I assure myself I'll study my way across the Pacific and pack my law books. Ernesto, another American, and I are the only passengers. I earn my keep with the crew doing odd jobs, mostly schlepping stuff. In 1975, the world is a very different place. I must have had a passport, but all I remember is breezing through immigration with the crew. It's the rainy season, hot and muggy. We make a beeline for the coliseum in Quezon City, a huge domed structure about 10 miles north of Manilla. The streets are jam-packed, electricity crackles like heat lightning in the air, stores and stands are hawking Ali memorabilia. I don't hear much English, but it doesn't matter; it never matters with Ali fans. We check into a dive hotel and hit the streets.

We clamber to our seats for the 10:00 a.m. start. Already stifling hot, the dome's aluminum roof traps humidity, converting the giant arena into a howling, sweating pressure cooker packed with seething fans, a good many drunk on excitement adrenalin, and the free-flowing tuba (coconut wine) and bootleg whiskey. The legendary animosity between the two men, grounded in Ali's insulting Frazier as an "Uncle Tom," "a gorilla," and worse, is palpable. Frazier will later say he prayed to God for the strength to kill Ali in the ring. It almost happens; they pound round after round, Frazier's thunderous left hook staggers Ali in the sixth round. Angelo Dundee screams for him to drop the ineffective rope-a-dope defense. Toe-to-toe exchanges dominate the eighth and ninth rounds. The crowd is in a frenzy as Ali lands punch after punch to Frazier's head, leaving his left eye swollen and shut. It's so hot at ringside that all the icepacks trainer Eddie Futch needs to treat Frazier's eye melt.

Somehow Frazier answers the bell for the 13th and 14th rounds, taking a tremendous beating; at one point his mouth guard flies across the canvas. "This is the closest I've ever been to dying!" Ali gasps to Dundee. In Frazier's corner, Futch has seen enough. Over Joe's objections, he signals referee Carlos Padilla Jr. that the fight is over. Ironically, it turns out that after the 14th round, Ali signaled his cornerman to cut his gloves off.

We leave the stadium exhausted. Prizefights connect on a primitive, emotional level independent of our conscious minds. I literally feel I was in the ring with Ali enduring Frazier's haymakers. We spend a day among the wild partygoers in Cubao

City but the craziness does little in terms of recuperation. Finally it dawns on me, I'm 8,000 miles from home. Law school classes are already underway.

May 9, 1981. The Champ is in town.

"He's doing this benefit for Muscular Dystrophy," I tell Elisa. "What time can you get off?"

"Bobby, I'm busy!"

"How busy can you be?" (She manages a bank.) "Can you get Anita to cover for you?"

"I'll see if she's free. Hang on."

Anita Byrd is the head teller at the First Georgia Bank branch Elisa manages.

"She's free," Elisa says.

"Great!" Anita is so great that I hire her to run my law office. A job she does very well for many years.

I'm there when Ali fights Larry Holmes in Las Vegas in 1980. I sneak into the weigh-in with my buddy and now lifelong friend, Ed Kanner. I hide in plain sight under a baseball cap with a big NBC peacock logo. I hear Ali whisper to Angelo Dundee, "I just don't feel right." I'd been at the "Drama in Bahamas" fiasco in December 1981 when Trevor Berbick, the European champion, literally refused to enter the ring until he received his $1 million guarantee in cash. Elisa understands this whole Ali craziness—and my Mantle craziness—firsthand. I'd traveled to New Orleans with Andy Berger and Jay Schneider (insane Ali fans) in the fall of 1978 to watch Ali beat a much younger Leon Spinks and regain the heavyweight championship. Before the fight, Andy, a husband of one of Elisa's sorority sisters, and I sneak into the arena to make sure the ropes are not too loose for Ali to work his rope-a-dope magic.

May 9, 1981.

In the 1980s, midtown Atlanta has one decent hotel, Colony Square, the same joint Irwin, Elisa, and I crashed to attend Mickey Mantle's memorable golf banquet. Here we are, a banker and a lawyer, skulking in the lobby, watching the elevators, sizing up guests as they enter and leave. No luck.

"What are we gonna do?"

"He's gotta be in the Presidential Suite."

"Come on!"

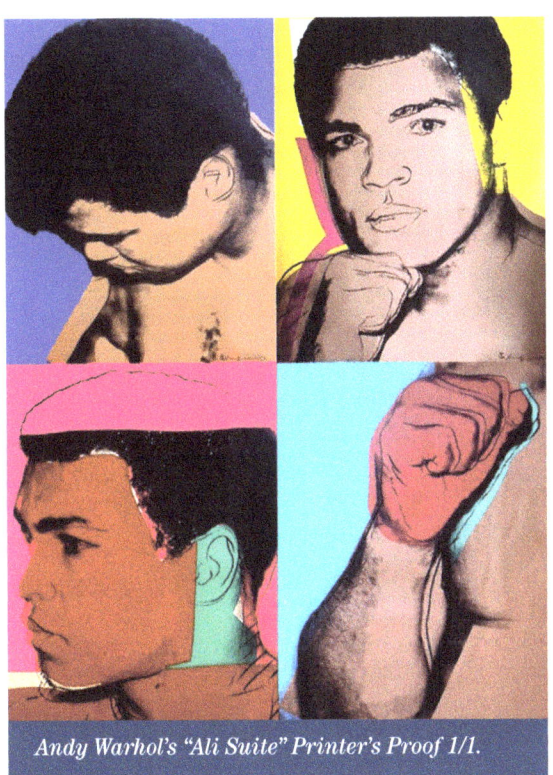

Andy Warhol's "Ali Suite" Printer's Proof 1/1.

In the elevator, you need a key to get to the concierge floor. Someone gets off, we follow, hesitate a moment, and then step into the hall. It's like the *Let's Make A Deal* TV show, only instead of three doors, there are thirty. Instead of Monty Hall, there's a concierge to avoid.

Then, miraculously, I hear his voice, that soft, resonant whisper that is unmistakably Ali. One of the doors to his suite is open a crack. Elisa giggles.

"Bring me a towel." A voice that is like no other voice.

I walk up to the door, leaning on it so it opens a little more. There he is, dressed in a sweatsuit, lying in bed on a pile of towels, peeling the first of a pile of oranges.

"Excuse me, Champ, how you doing?" I was never shy.

Eye Contact: Thrill of a lifetime getting to know Ali.

"Fine...fine."

Apparently, it's the most ordinary thing in the world for a perfect stranger to walk into your hotel suite.

"Mind if I come in?"

"Come on in. Bring your pretty lady with you."

Two men are in the suite's other room. One I recognize as Ali's younger brother, Rahman.

Elisa sits in a chair by the door. I look around; not finding a suitable place to sit, I plop down on the bed next to Ali. For a moment, the two of us just lie there, easy as Jim and Huckleberry Finn on a Delta riverbank. Then I start talking. I blurt out everything in two minutes: how "Danny Ginsburg and I were the only two kids pulling for you in the seventh grade...how insanely hot the Manilla Dome was...how Andy Berger (another lawyer) and I checked the ropes for you at the second Spinks' fight at the New Orleans Superdome to make sure you had plenty of bounce. How Trevor Berbick kept you waiting in the ring—I saw it—until he got his money. How you won that match." By now, I'm elbowing him, kidding around, kibitzing. I tell him, "My father is a Marine who thinks you're a draft dodger. I kind of understand, but I never really understand. I don't care. I loved you unconditionally!"

This is true. When I was a kid, Mickey Mantle was a cartoon Superman. Ali was never that. Ali was real, a flesh and blood human being. Ali is current. Which love is deeper? Not even close.

"I'll never understand your religious thing," I add, half to cover my embarrassment.

"What's so hard for you to understand?" he whispers. "Are you Jewish?"

"Yeah."

"You don't have a problem understanding burning bushes that don't consume themselves? Christians don't have a problem understanding a man rising up from the dead? Mormons have chariots coming down from the sky. No one seems to have a problem. They all have a problem with my stuff. We have flying saucers that are going to pick us up, bring us to heaven." (The "Mother Wheel," a UFO embodying the purifying presence of God that, according to Nation of Islam theology, appeared to Elijah Muhammad and Louis Farrakhan.)

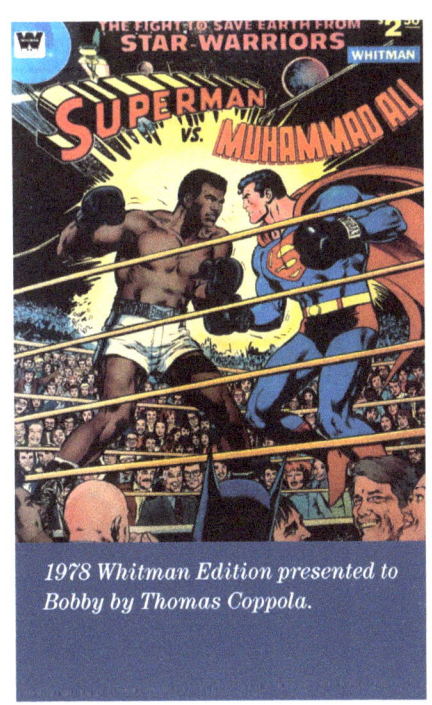

1978 Whitman Edition presented to Bobby by Thomas Coppola.

"What's crazy about that idea, and not crazy about a chariot with flying horses?"

"You got a point."

"What do you do?" he asks, flipping me an orange slice.

"I'm a lawyer."

For the rest of my life, anytime I'm in Ali's presence, my official name is "Lawyer."

"Lawyer," he whispers, his hands encircling an orange, this world that we're in, compared to what's to come, is like sticking your finger in the ocean. The water that's left on your finger when you pull it out, that amount of water, compared to the whole ocean, is our life here on earth compared to what's to come."

I'm silent.

At that moment, we're interrupted.

"Champ, we got a problem," says Rahman.

"What?"

"They lost your luggage. You've got nothing to wear!"

Unperturbed, Ali goes back to his oranges. "Get the Lawyer to take care of it."

I call down to the concierge and ask to be connected to the nearest tuxedo rental place. It's not far, by the Georgia Tech campus, but time is a factor.

"I have the champion of the world here," I begin. "He's lost his luggage and he's got a thing tonight. He needs a tuxedo."

"Bring him on over."

"I can't."

Imagine the scene: Muhammad Ali walking into a store as if he were an ordinary human and The Varsity, the famous and always-packed hot dog emporium, right across the street.

"Have someone come over to the Colony Square. The concierge will handle it. Bring the biggest size you got, and your sewing kit."

A half-hour later, a woman shows up, a middle-age African American, very businesslike given the circumstances.

She slides the tux out of its wrapper.

"This is the biggest size we've got, but it's not as big as this guy."

Ali laughs boyishly, like he's somehow grown too big and now he's being disciplined by his grandmother. He is six foot three, has an 81-inch reach, and is a little overweight, well, overweight for him. She goes into the other room, takes all the hems out, and she sews the thing by hand to make it as big as she can around the waist.

"I've spread this jacket as far as I can," she says.

He gets up, takes the tux from her, and goes into the bathroom.

He comes out. He can't button the jacket. He can barely zip up the pants. It's a disaster!

The seamstress is nervous. Reality—working with the most famous man on the planet and his tux doesn't fit!—is setting in. I can see any number of folks I know—prima donnas, ordinary shmoes, good guys, who'd say, "I can't go to an event like this. It fits me like a f..king disease!"

"Is it okay?" the seamstress manages.

Ali being a good sport with me and great friends and fellow fight judges Ed Kanner (left) and Irwin Deutsch (right).

The Champ turns from his mirror image. He turns to the tiny woman standing in front of him. A woman who had done her very best and had come up short.

"Momma," he whispers. "It's perfect!" He gives her a big hug.

In that moment, he was as great as great could be.

Spring 2005.

Somehow I'm 55 years old and on a tour of colleges with my son Zachary. One of our stops is tiny Bates College in Lewiston, Maine, a town very familiar to me though I've never been here. Zack, impressed with the welcoming atmosphere and pastoral campus, decides to meet with the admissions committee.

I drive over to St. Dominic's Arena on Birch Street, scene of the 1965 Sonny Liston/Muhammad Ali rematch. The hangar-like structure is not so much deserted—it's a sometime convention center—as haunted by bright shadows from the past. Here, for a very brief moment, a struggling mill town staged a heavyweight championship boxing match on three weeks' notice and the world showed up. Here, brash 23-year-old Cassius Clay transformed into monumental Muhammad Ali. Here, the mysterious "phantom punch" that laid Sonny Liston low at 1:40 in the first round—fans were still making their way to their seats, tubs of popcorn in hand—would be debated for the next half-century. Sinatra was here, as well as Elizabeth Taylor, Joe Louis, James J. Braddock, Howard Cosell, and the whole media circus Ali would command for the rest of his life.

"Mamma, it's perfect." Colony Square Hotel, May 9, 1981.

He has 10 years to live. He has developed Parkinson's disease, surely traceable to the trauma endured in the ring. There is no more poetry, no more rhyming, no more "I Am The Greatest!" theatrics. It occurs to me I've spent years of my life hanging on to the man's every word, following him to the ends of the earth, studying his performances as other men study Shakespeare. Ali is far more than an athlete. Larger than life, he's a heroic figure.

And I've been blessed to know him.

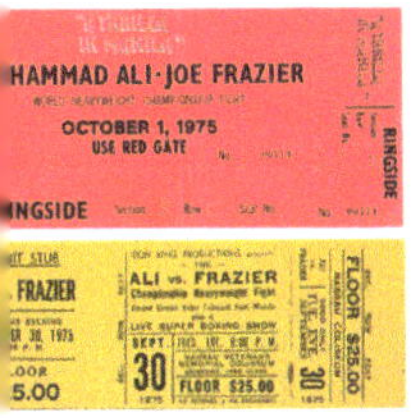

A lifetime of Ali memorabilia including Warhol's "Ali Suite" Printer's Proof 1/1 and rare international Ali figurine telephone presented to me by cousins Esta, Todd, and Donna Goodman.

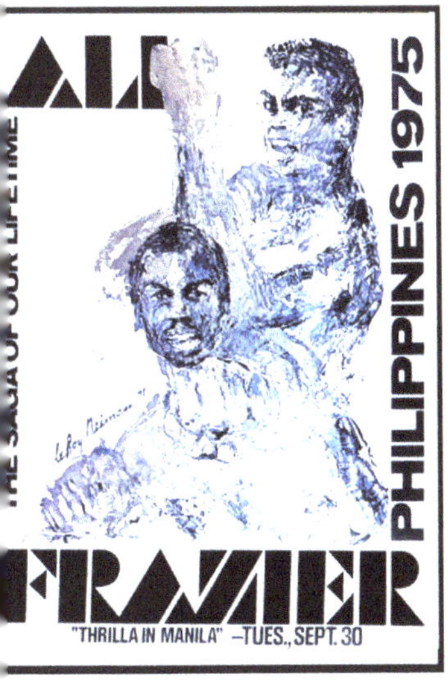

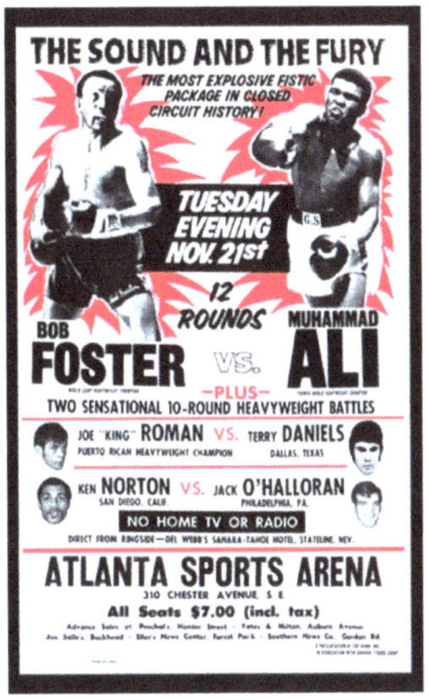

BOBBY EZOR | ORDINARY LIFE IS EXTRAORDINARY

Chapter 11

Like the bar in *Cheers*, Jerry Farber's club is a place where lifelong friendships are made.

1973

My first time in Atlanta, a cabbie tells me Johnny's Hideaway is a place to go. Given the clientele, Johnny's appears to be a geriatric singles bar in the corner of a strip mall, but first impressions can be misleading. Like Jonathan Harker's arrival at Dracula's castle in Transylvania, I'm instantly surrounded by leering, lascivious women with lips the color of blood, some my mother's age. Rather than my soul, they carry off my wallet. Next time, I venture farther north to The Lark and The Dove, a jazz club on the "Perimeter," whatever that is. Here the up-tempo chords of Duke Ellington's "Take the 'A' Train" greet me like a breath of spring at the door. At the piano, fingers flying, is a lanky, sad-faced guy who turns out to be the comedian. This sounds like the beginning of a bad joke: "A Jewish guy from New Jersey walks into a bar..."

Funnyman Jerry Farber performing his classic University of Georgia "Mr. Grungeballs" routine, complete with redneck teeth and UGA cap. To their credit, the most avid Georgia fans laughed the hardest!

What I don't know is that Jerry Farber and I will become dear friends and hit the high and low notes in each other's lives for the next half-century.

It turns out Jerry is the brother of a guy whose name rings a bell: Barry Farber is a conservative and very popular NYC talk-radio host, a guy my father and his cronies appreciate. Barry, who died at age 90, is still considered one of the great all-time radio talents; Jerry Farber plays the piano. Barry spoke 20 languages and captained his college wrestling team. No easy task being this guy's kid brother. Jerry's signature comedic riff—"How 'Bout Dem Dawgs!" involves plastic buckteeth and a trip inside the head of a good ol' boy Georgia fan—is still hysterical the 50th time you hear it, but his fans are still waiting for the next act. Jerry is a sensitive and brilliant underachiever, to the point of self-torment; a magnet for women, though not the cheerleaders he's always lusted after, but high-mileage divorcees who hang out in bars in the wee hours of the morning. He's a degenerate gambler, famous for betting big time on his beloved Tar Heels; infamous for tapping a circle of friends who love him unconditionally for cash to stave off the next disaster. Bookies cling to him like pilot fish, a fixture at his performances as much as drunks and hangers-on.

Soulful jazz pianist Jerry Farber favors me with a private cover of the great Earl Garner's "Teach Me Tonight."

Of course, we become instant friends. All these years later, his humor still tickles me. The jokes are lame, I know the punchlines by heart, but I can't help myself. Like his idol, Woody Allen, Jerry's comedy is driven by his ever-expanding neuroses—he's a walking *DSM (Diagnostic and Statistical Manual)*, the bible of mental dysfunction. Anxiety, check; insecurity, check; paranoia, check; irresponsibility, check; and of course, hypochondria, double-check. Years ago at a roast, photographer and long-suffering Farber friend Chip Simone came up with the perfect inscription for Jerry's tombstone:

"You see, I told you I didn't feel good!"

His financial difficulties are legendary. Like Wimpy in the *Popeye* cartoons, it's always, "I'll gladly pay you Tuesday for a hamburger today." To be honest, I never gave Jerry money that I expected to get back. I'm sure that's true of most of Jerry's friends, but loan sharks want their money, which always makes for some interesting late-night performances. Many times, our buddy Seth Kirschenbaum, a savvy criminal defense attorney, saved Jerry from himself.

Of course, his money problems work their way into Jerry's bits, and by extension, our lives. Years ago, I attended many Atlanta Hawks home games. My season tickets were at half-court, and as I made my way to my seat—usually late—I'd walk past broadcast engineer John Kramer. This happened so often John and I got into this little kibitz involving shoulder taps and feints. One night, I mention that I'd grabbed a bite to eat with this guy, Jerry Farber. "I know Jerry Farber!" Kramer says, pulling off his headphones. He pulls his wallet out of his back pocket and there's this old scribbled IOU. He'd lent Jerry a couple hundred bucks about 20 years ago, and needless to say, he's still waiting.

So I tell John when Farber is doing a roast or birthday party. Kramer begins showing up. He'd take the IOU out of his pigskin wallet and pass it around. It caused such a stir and so many laughs that Jerry incorporated John into the act. That IOU became more valuable than the money. It became a collector's item.

Jerry's life has been rich in irony. In his twenties, he balks at joining the family garment business. Jerry is unwilling to play a Southern Willie Loman, so he goes into comedy. In his thirties and forties, he's forever on the brink of the breakthrough appearance on Carson, Letterman, or Leno, and it always seems to fall through, sometimes because of Jerry's irrational fear of not being good enough. Like the wandering Jew of myth, he spends these years in the desert of the Southern comedy club circuit, the rubber chicken circuit, the corporate banquet circuit, emceeing charitable functions and campus gigs, logging as many as 200 shows a year in a battered 2002 Nissan, selling himself to the lowest bidder.

"I did a fundraiser for a library at Auburn (University) that burned down three weeks ago," he confides. "Both books were destroyed. And one of them hadn't even been colored in yet."

In 1989, Jerry opens an upscale comedy club on Pharr Road in Buckhead, showcasing future stars like Brett Butler, Jeff Foxworthy, and the Indigo Girls.

Fans, old and new, line up outside the door. Jerry, being the iconoclast, bans patrons from smoking. He was decades ahead of his time, but drinking and smoking are de rigueur in nightclubs. His backers' investments go up in smoke. Personal life? Jerry stumbles through three marriages and a daisy chain of one-night stands and failed relationships. He decides to become a first-time father in his sixties. You can almost hear the jokes: "The patriarch Abraham walks into a bar..." Like the biblical Abraham, Jerry Farber is blessed with a son when most men his age are grandfathers looking back at their lives.

That son, Joshua, is Jerry's great joy.

I no longer question—in fact, I now embrace—the tsuris that is so much a part of Jerry's life. This is what friends are for. The guy can't pass an abandoned dog or cat on the street without bringing the creature home. A fact that's very apparent when you visit. "Jerry, open the goddamn windows!" I shout. "I can't," he says, "the pigeons will escape!" In recent years, I spent many hours and much hands-on labor helping put together a comedy venue—another showcase for Jerry—on a property owned by a man so difficult to deal with that Job would have thrown up his hands in despair. The club opens to great fanfare—"Jerry Farber is back!"—but in 2015, the landlord's never-ending intransigence sinks it.

Jerry is famously pain-averse. So it's not surprising that he avoids dental appointments for decades, to the point where his friends complain that it's hard to "share an egg roll" with him, i.e., his teeth are falling out of his mouth. I tap into the Jerry Farber reservoir of goodwill and, sure enough, the top dental practice in Atlanta agrees to do the work pro bono. Now comes the hard part: Jerry misses appointment after appointment, a disruptive and costly thing for a busy practice. He begins to leave me tortured phone messages: He's "afraid...nervous...uncomfortable...

bummed out...scared...sorry."

Excuses run off his tongue like one-liners.

I give up, thinking this could actually be the end of Jerry Farber. Not long after, he moves to Columbus, Georgia. And soon enough, he's entertaining another generation of fans at Ma Bella's and The Loft. The plastic buckteeth are back in action.

Jerry's No. 1 fan supporting him in his ill-fated run for mayor in 1985.

Over the years, as I've watched these things unfold, I've come to know Jerry as I know myself. He's a good man—generous, passionate, and sensitive to a fault—but pulled by unfathomable currents in different directions. A "comedian" who can capture the longing, loneliness, and bittersweet in life. A poster boy for the never-ending decisions, indecisions, revisions, roads taken or not taken, and often regretted, we all must face. An artist who never stops giving of himself, who in his eighties finds himself still unable to enjoy the fruits of his labor.

Jerry's great genius is that he can absorb this existential pain, wrap it in shiny tinsel and bows, and like Pagliacci, smile when he's gasping on the inside. If you imagine that in our greed-driven, materialistic world, people would flee from such a man, you are wrong. Jerry is literally beloved by an intensely loyal circle of Atlanta friends—Nancy Habif, Scott Kleber, Jerry Lindenberg (RIP), Johnny Porrazzo, Chip Simone, David Dermer, Seth Kirschenbaum, Howard Osofsky, David Lowell—among them. Hundreds more in "the business" and thousands more if you count his fans.

And, of course, me. He does this bit whenever I appear at one of his performances:

"Bobby Ezor and I have been friends for 30, 35, 40, now 47 years. There is nothing that I wouldn't do for Bobby and there is nothing that Bobby wouldn't do for me. That is the nature of our friendship. (pause) I've never done anything for him, and he's never done anything for me!"

In truth, Jerry has given me the most valuable gift one human can give another: his time, his heart, and his love. Whether I was supporting a cause, marking a life cycle event, or simply in need of a pal, he was there. The best Jerry Farber performances have always been in private: whether a soulful rendition of an Erroll Garner tune on the beat-up old upright piano at his midtown home, or appreciating each other's ideas and experiences on hours-long, meaningful, thoughtful, and flat-out funny phone calls. Jerry has shared this sweetness with me, my family, and our friends. He showed up when I needed him: be it a fundraiser, an occasion to share our love for our parents, even providing part-time jobs for my sheltered kids to open their eyes to the real world. It was never for the money.

He has done this for so many people: used his life and sorrows, joys, and frustrations to provide the place, that sacred community, where lifelong friendships are nurtured and grown. I've come to realize Jerry never did anything for us and we never did anything for him—other than to learn to love unconditionally.

Chapter 12

"Time is a jet plane, it moves too fast."

Bob Dylan

Elisa and I renew our vows in Hanover Parish, Jamaica.

Somehow,

Elisa and I have been married almost seven years. Among the keys to our enduring relationship are humor, spontaneity, and the iron-clad commitment to never, ever end a day without saying "I love you." That last one is not as easy as it sounds. Sometimes "love" can feel like an icicle or a dagger, but we stick to it. One night, we're watching an episode of *Dallas*, the never-ending and insanely popular CBS potboiler. "I can't believe Bobby Ewing and Pamela got remarried!" Elisa exclaims tearfully. "And everybody is so happy!"

A moment later, she asks, "Would you remarry me?"

"Yes, of course," I say half-asleep. "I guess."

Spontaneity. Next day, I'm researching places where married couples remarry. There are the obvious ones: Niagara Falls, Las Vegas, and then, oddly, Hanover Parish, Jamaica.

"Let's get married in Jamaica!" I say arriving home after work. "Pack a white dress."

We arrive in Hanover Parish, on the island's northwest corner, and check into Round Hill, a boutique resort in Montego Bay. Our suite, with its sweeping view of the Caribbean, is owned by the William "Bill" Shea family, the same Bill Shea who was instrumental in returning a National League baseball team, the Mets, to New York City after the Dodgers and the Giants fled for California. We check in and soon we're heading over to Montego Bay in search of a marriage license. Percival Thompson III, the "Civil Registrar of Marriages," has a tiny second-floor office above a freight company down a back alley. The room is crudely divided into partitions, and we're herded into one. (I'm reminded of cattle being led into a slaughterhouse.) You can't see anybody outside your partition, but you can hear everything. What I hear, and occasionally glimpse, are numbers of middle-age white women and young Jamaican men applying for marriage licenses. Odd couples, who basically ignore each other until an official walks by, then, instantly, it's all smooches and hugs. The show of affection stops as quickly as an afternoon thunderstorm the moment the coast is clear. The only freight seemingly being shipped is citizenship.

Then it's our turn.

"What can I do for you?" Percival asks in his lilting accent.

"We want to get remarried."

He's reaching for the paperwork, when it hits him. "Are you married?"

"Yes. We're married. We want to get remarried."

"You can't get remarried if you're married."

"It's a romantic thing."

"No...no...no!"

"Why?"

"If you are already married, you can't get remarried."

We go back and forth like some mad Abbott and Costello routine. I sense our unseen audience of pretend newlyweds does not appreciate the spectacle.

"We just want to renew our vows," I say. Then I tell Percival about Bobby Ewing and Pamela. I can't be sure, but he seems to recognize *Dallas*.

"Let's start over," he says more patiently. "Are you married?"

"No."

"Good."

Percival tells me he must send a courier to Kingston for an official stamp to be affixed on our document. This will take a certain number of days.

"Days?"

"You can marry in ten days."

"Okay." We've come this far.

"Where will you celebrate your wedding?"

"Round Hill, right down the road."

"I'll marry you," he says, surprising me. "I don't always, but this time I will."

When the big day comes, Percival shows up with a bible and clerical collar. I've hired a photographer and a florist, and have made other arrangements for our wedding party. The Duchess of Milan; her husband, the Duke; and their polo-playing son happen to be staying at the resort. She graciously agrees to give Elisa away. I suspect none of our fellow guests realize this is our second marriage, unless they've been watching *Dallas*. For three days, all our meals appear mysteriously at our door—custom allows newlyweds sufficient time to consummate their union and are showered with every amenity. Bobby Ewing and Pamela would be proud.

Life, of course, is not just apples and honey. A few years later, we decide to get pregnant and run headlong into infertility problems. We tell ourselves it's not uncommon, we're still young, we have time. As the poet T.S. Eliot writes, "And time yet for a hundred indecisions, and for a hundred visions and revisions…." In the next years, many of our married friends give birth and we register the brisses and baptisms and baby showers. Soon, those newborns are starting school and we're still on the outside looking in. We find an infertility doctor, Joe B. Massey, M.D., and follow his guidance to the letter. This is a season of hormonal injections and timed ovulations, of hasty visits to a downtown hotel halfway from our offices. Anything but romantic, but we try. I send Elisa flowers and candy; she tells me she pretends we're having an affair, but legally. More years go by. Now, we're in our mid-thirties. And then we're on to in vitro procedures, three or four, each a cycle of hope, heartbreak, and resolve. I can't imagine how anyone wouldn't quit, but Elisa's fierce tenacity inspires me, even in the off-putting parts, when I have to go into a room and produce a specimen. We've built this bond—we could go through hell and make the best of it—that makes us inseparable and strange as it sounds, makes our marriage stronger.

As I recall, Elisa produced three eggs in the cycle; most women have 10 to 15 after ovulation. Massey's team fertilized all three in test tubes, but at his suggestion we decide to freeze one. The first two fail to thrive. We were down to one. I could say it was like Mickey Mantle up in the bottom of the ninth with two outs and two strikes, and the game on the line, but it wasn't like that, not at all. It was simpler and purer and humbling: Life itself being formed before our eyes.

We get so lucky—Zachary comes along, the first male in Dr. Massey's long practice to be born of a thawed egg. For his first birthday, we decide to celebrate at Fox Theater's flamboyant Egyptian Ballroom. The party is dedicated to the "Young at Heart"—Elisa and I and all our friends who'd been with us through the struggle. Zachary makes a brief appearance. There are acrobats on unicycles, a carousel, mimes, guys on stilts, and stations stocked with treats all kids love—cheeseburgers and ice cream sundaes. Everyone—these baby boomer doctors and lawyers and accountants—shows up as a childhood fantasy figure: Popeye and Olive Oyl, Raggedy Ann and Andy, Elisa in pigtails and freckles.

Me? Who else but Pee Wee Herman.

The story doesn't end there. Heartened by the seeming miracle of Zachary's birth, in the years ahead, Elisa and I make two more in vitro attempts, both heartrending. The first ends quickly; the second results in what seems like a successful pregnancy—two eggs are fertilized and implanted. Now, we start thinking about kids' rooms and furnishings and the dozens of things that go along with a suddenly expanding family. We decide we need a roomier house. Elisa makes it to the third trimester—31 weeks—when things go wrong. She goes into premature labor and is hospitalized for more than two weeks. Hoping to give our babies time to reach viability in the womb, our obstetrician prescribes powerful stabilizing drugs that trigger terrible hallucinations. Our twins, who weigh barely more than a pound each, are delivered by C-section and rushed to the neonatal unit and placed in incubators. I'm told it's unlikely they will survive, and if they do survive, they will be physically and mentally incapacitated. Here, Rabbi Arnold Goodman (you'll meet him in another chapter) guides us with honesty, wisdom, and compassion. When the time comes, the decision to take them off life support is not easy, but it's obvious.

Our options are narrowing. I'd always had issues with adoption. I don't know why. But one day I burst into the house and say, "Let's adopt!" I still don't know what caused the light to go off, maybe maturity, or memories of loneliness as a boy, or the pure joy Elisa and I take in parenting. We put the word out. One day, Irvin Rabinowitz, a friend who works as an accountant for an adoption agency, calls and says, "I know you guys are thinking about adoption, and I happen to know there's a baby girl who's going to be up for adoption in the coming days. Are you guys interested?"

Elisa and I are both on the call. Without hesitation, we both blurt, "Yes!"

The fact that our new baby is female adds to our delight. We're already into "frogs and snails and puppy dog tails," now it's time for "sugar and spice." Danielle is born in Washington, D.C. Because states have differing guidelines for adoption, we travel to Little Rock, Arkansas, where the D.C. adoption agency has a satellite office. With three-year-old Zack in tow, we check into the historic Capitol Hotel—I have an imprinted bar of soap as a keepsake—and wait for the foster family to present us with our soon-to-be daughter. They take a leap of faith and leave Danielle with us for the weekend. Then the four of us—this newly formed nuclear family—stroll over to the courthouse for the adoption procedure. At the close, the presiding judge asks, "Is there anything else anyone would like to add?"

Zachary pipes up. "I want to keep my baby sister for all the days and all the nights."

The judge orders, "Let the record reflect that Zachary can have his baby sister for all the days and all the nights."

In the summer of 2020, that little boy, Zachary, himself a lawyer, and his wife Lara, welcome our first grandchild, Samuel Goodrich Ezor, into the world. That little girl, Danielle Rebecca Ezor, now a brilliant art history scholar working on her PhD, welcomes Sam with overflowing love and joy.

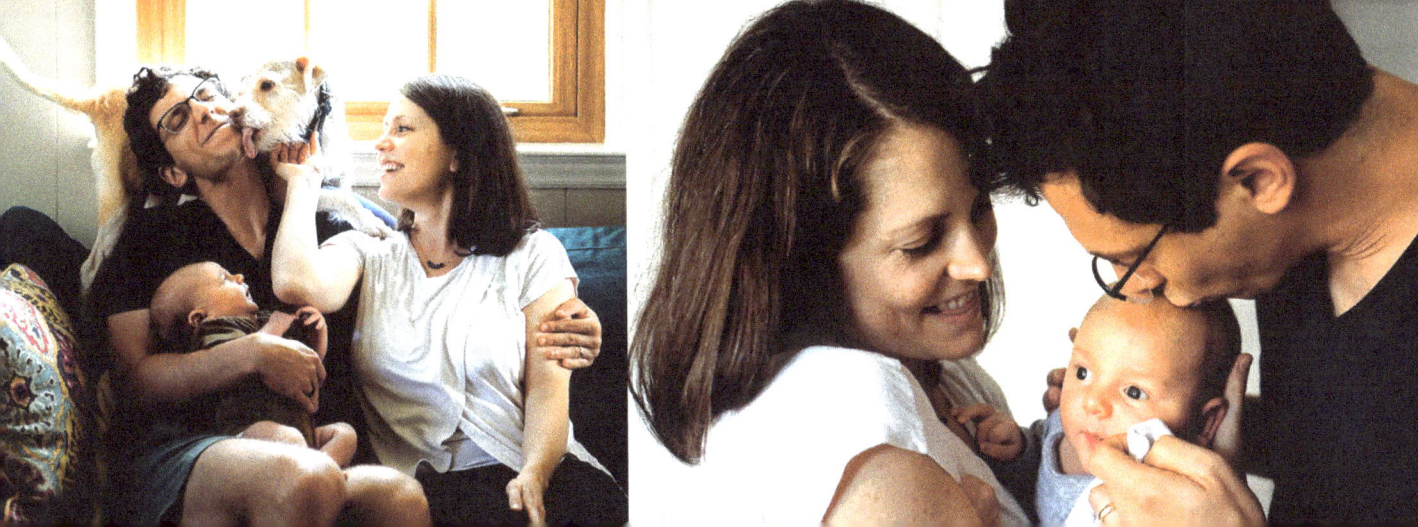

Bobby and Elisa, daughter Dani, and son Zack. Zack with childhood sweetheart/wife Lara and our grandson Sammy.

BOBBY EZOR | ORDINARY LIFE IS EXTRAORDINARY

Chapter 13

"It's the way you ride the trail that counts."

Gene Autry, "Happy Trails"

Men's Senior Hardball

Bobby scoring and stealing.

North Atlanta Mustang Team Shot.

Coach Don Valentine signs me up.

Tony Cameron and I take in one of many. Fun to go to the game with somebody who has walked the walk.

Me with a five-day growth; it's bad luck to shave when on a winning streak.

Teammate #14 and great friend Jay Smith with my son Zachary, 1997. You won't find a better mentor.

Practical joker Cam Killebrew (Hall of Famer Harmon's Killebrew's son). Nice catch!

Head

Coach Valentine autographed ball.

on over to Jim Hearn's Driving Range.

The command is softened by a tickle of mischief and an east Tennessee twang, but even on the phone it's clear that Lieutenant Colonel McDonald Valentine (Ret.) is comfortable giving orders.

"Sure thing, Coach!"

I jump in my car and head over to a driving range—it has seen better days—shoehorned among aging apartment complexes, body shops, garages, and scores of Chinese, Korean, and Vietnamese restaurants and groceries seemingly popped up overnight on Buford Highway. This is Chamblee, Atlanta's Asia Town, referred to with genteel racism as "Chambodia." An unlikelier place for a baseball clinic I can't imagine.

I'm 39, married with a three-year-old son, a successful lawyer, but I cling to this birthday present from my wife Elisa—10 lessons with a legendary baseball coach recommended by my friend "Stash"—with the excitement of, well, a 10-year-old. Coach McDonald "Don" Valentine is a decorated Vietnam veteran trained in PsyOps (psychological warfare), a poet, a calligrapher, a philosopher, and as I'm about to learn, one of the most talented and eccentric people I'll ever meet.

When I arrive at Jim Hearn's—careful to avoid being beaned by a mishit golf ball—I head over to the batting cages where a crowd is gathered. There's a guy lying on his back holding a baseball bat upright like a flagpole. The pitching machine is firing balls at him. He's making contact lying prone. Consistent contact like a hockey goalie fending off breakaways. Then he gets up and hits a couple of homers left-handed, then switches over to the other side and hits a couple of homers right-handed. He takes out a BB gun and has onlookers toss Styrofoam cups in the air—plink...plink... plink—he plugs each one.

It's a circus.

Don Valentine is 43 years old. Founder, manager, coach, and face of the North Atlanta Mustangs, a storied semi-pro baseball team where I'll flesh out a lifelong fantasy for the coming 10 years. When I meet him, he's overweight, the proverbial "unmade bed," scratching out a living selling Mustang paraphernalia out of the trunk of his car to middle-aged Peter Pans like me who refuse to grow up. But there is so much more to Don Valentine: He was born in Alabama, attended high school in Florida—his father was a peripatetic naval officer—Don won a full scholarship to the University of Miami and later transferred to the University of Tennessee as a junior. There, an ROTC commitment sent him off to Vietnam, the familiar story of another gifted player who never made it to the show. Instead, Valentine's love grew into obsession: He bounced around, hoping to attract the attention of a major league team, scouted for the White Sox. Over time, he realized his gift was coaching, understanding the game at the granular level, knowing intimately how winning baseball is played, and passing on this knowledge—and other oddball life lessons—to generations of players.

I can recite chapter and verse of Mickey Mantle's career. I've attended hundreds of Yankees and Braves games, but having season tickets behind home plate is not baseball. I've literally played a thousand softball games at the Atlanta JCC. I'm athletic, quick, wiry, and possess good reflexes, but I've never played hardball—well, except for summer camp where a foul tip to the shin can make a boy cry. Valentine is about to make that abundantly clear.

"Let's see what you got," he says.

We throw the ball around. "This is not softball," he says, as if I might have somehow missed that. "This is the real thing."

I figure I'll catch on.

Next Sunday, he starts me at third base. Balls go whistling by me. He keeps me there for three consecutive games. In Vietnam, Valentine was a special forces instructor; his students guys dropped behind enemy lines. It's life and death every time they go out. That's what this feels like. With every crack of the bat, I'm sure I'm going to stop a line drive with my teeth. Same thing at the plate: The first three games, three of my ten precious lessons, I bat nine times and strike out nine times. And these guys are not throwing 90 mph, more like 80 mph, mixed in with real curveballs and sliders.

"Holy shit!" I think. "I'm in way over my head!"

I'm demoralized, but that's the point. Psychological warfare. "Now Big Shot, you can take all that softball and stuff it!" he says. "If you really wanna learn to play baseball..."

"Sir, yes Sir!" I shout.

Braves Hall of Famer Phil Niekro, then coaching the all-women's Silver Bullets, throws me and teammate Dr. Mark Brenner a knuckleball.

I buy everything out of the trunk of his car. Every gimmick and gadget that might help me excel. Tees and sawed-off golf clubs with flashlights taped to them so I can follow the arc of my swing to maximize my hitting. On Coach's advice, I build a major league batting cage in my backyard, complete with a state-of-the-art Jugs™ pitching machine capable of throwing 80 mph fastballs and curves. I plant full-length mirrors around our bed, stand on top of the mattress, and take 150 swings studying myself intimately before I go to sleep. Elisa has created a monster. Then with Coach's support, I convert our 4,000-square-foot basement into a high-speed Wiffle® ball stadium. And soon enough, 45-year-old executives are showing up to play Wiffle ball at my house.

"Practice doesn't make perfect," Coach Valentine harps. "Only perfect practice makes perfect!" The venerable Vince Lombardi chestnut is one of a collection of aphorisms he carries around like a bottomless tin of chewing tobacco. "We can only have one commander in the dugout!" is another. (I'm a lawyer. Sitting next to me is the president of Cox Communications, a multibillion dollar conglomerate. And here's this guy living out of a car acting like General Patton. Needless to say, we sit straight as ramrods.) There's more: "If you don't get dirty, you haven't played the game. Take care of your equipment and your equipment will take care of you. Stand tall to maul the ball. O is a killer, V is a thriller. Pocket to pocket makes it rocket." I'm psyched up, but Valentine doesn't let me play again—after those first three games—until the season is half over and I've bought 20 more lessons.

Why am I doing this? Why am I so eager to devote time and money to what is ultimately, a kids' game? What is so intoxicating? Am I, as my friend Chip Simone likes to say, the eternal "fish" played by every con artist? Not at all. I've thought about this over the years. I've chased the same thing my whole life—friendship, experience, challenge, fun. I want to be part of the great American pastime depicted in The Pride of the Yankees, Field of Dreams, The Rookie. I have been a spectator, I have idols (Mickey Mantle), but this is my first real taste of the game—the smell of freshly cut infield grass, the crack of a bat, a fastball slapping into a catcher's mitt. It's seductive. It's alluring. I want to play before I'm reduced to racquetball and riding very expensive bikes on skinny tires.

Coach Valentine understands this—it's an American story. In simplest terms, he teaches me to play baseball at a level I've never imagined possible. When Coach adds "perfect" to our never-ending batting and fielding practice (staying on the balls of your feet, positioning your body) a better than average player gets really good. In tournaments, I bat against All-Star Bill "Spaceman" Lee and Cy Young Award-winner Mike Marshall. (Yes, these guys really play in this league.) I have a shot at them because Coach has taught me well. I practice bunting until I'm the best on the team. I'll never be a power hitter, but I can hit .300 and get on base. I lead our team two years in a row in stolen bases. A kamikaze baserunner, I show up at my law office too many Monday mornings, shins seeping blood through my pinstriped suits. I make games happen.

We play on high school fields, in north Atlanta at Oglethorpe University, and at other area colleges. Many of my teammates are former college ballplayers, some ex-minor leaguers. Most of us are in our forties, but one relief pitcher we face, Jim Tyler, 72, is still suckering batters with his junk balls. I play alongside CEOs, investment bankers, lawyers, physicians, owners of car dealerships, most of them very competitive guys. Coach Valentine gets a kick watching these masters of the universe quake in their boots when facing real pitching, and, heaven forbid, striking out. "Baseball is a game where failure must be coped with," he'd remind us. "The greatest hitters of all time make out two of every three at bats." Try to convince a preening corporate CEO to embrace those stats.

Fields of Dreams: Coach V taught me all I know.

We're good enough—another tribute to Valentine—to qualify for regional and national tournaments. There are road trips to Kissimmee, Florida, and Tempe, Arizona. We play against Russians, the Virgin Islands champions, and two games against a Phil Niekro-managed team of 20-something women dressed in A League of Their Own vintage uniforms. These women are tough. The blisters and raspberries on their legs are proof. We come away with a split. Annoyed, Niekro complains we're playing too hard. Coach Valentine: "We're 50 years old and we're out to win."

Camaraderie, mischief, and fun are part of the game, forged, not as General Douglas MacArthur declared, on "fields of friendly strife," but in dugouts, over drinks, wisecracks, practical jokes, and the occasional miraculous play. One of my favorite baseball films is The Natural starring Robert Redford as star-crossed Roy Hobbs who performs supernatural feats on the baseball diamond. Valentine's Mustangs compete in the Roy Hobbs Senior World Series Baseball Tournament held each year in Fort Meyers, Florida. Without fail, some unheralded schlub hits a titanic home run or makes a miraculous catch and is the hero of the tournament.

That's the magic of baseball. My Hobbesian moment comes at an invitational holiday tournament at Oglethorpe University's Anderson Field in Atlanta. I've been invited by Tony Cameron, a superlative college player, once a top pro-prospect. I'm a scrub, but the rules mandate everyone on the roster must play three innings. My teammates stick me in right field where they figure I can do the least amount of harm.

Sure enough, some guy hits a towering fly ball. I'm running, running. The ball is bending into a dogleg. Now, I'm running at full speed—the umpire following me—and I make the catch of my life, a Roy Hobbs catch, totally extended, the ball settling like a snow cone into the tip of my mitt. I go tumbling, crashing into the wall, somehow hanging onto the ball. The umpire raises his arm.

Bobby and Tony Cameron in 1996. Check out those waistlines!

"Out!"

This is all visible to my teammates in the third-base dugout. I remember dusting myself off, feeling really great, and heading toward our dugout. Not one guy says one single word. They ignore me as if the play never happened. The game continues. The game is over. We all go home. No one ever says a word about the greatest catch I ever made.

Then six months later, I'm walking across the West Paces Ferry parking lot to the Wender & Roberts Pharmacy near my house. Cam Killebrew, son of Hall of Famer Harmon Killebrew, is coming out of the store. Cam was in the dugout the day I made The Catch. I haven't seen him since. I'm walking in; he's walking out. He passes me, brushes me with his shoulder as he walks by, but he doesn't say a word. He stops. He turns around.

"Hey, Bobby."

I turn around.

"Nice catch," he says.

They'd given me the classic baseball cold shoulder. Cold shoulders, locker room rituals, rookie hazing, superstitions, practical jokes, and pranks—the "hot foot," underwear stuffed with peanut butter, live snakes hidden in lockers—are traditions running back to modern-day baseball's late-19th century roots.

By now, it's clear it's the camaraderie, as captured in the Boys of Summer, Ball Four, Summer of '49, Munson, and other baseball classics, that I'm seeking. What I've been seeking my whole life. In my forties, thanks to Coach Valentine, I forge new friendships—Tony Cameron and Jay Smith foremost among them—that are still vibrant 25 years later.

Jay Smith, the Mustangs' left fielder—I settle in at center field—is the most decent man I've ever known. Born in modest circumstances in Cincinnati, Jay rises from beat reporter in Dayton, Ohio, to president of the vast Cox Communications empire and its flagship newspaper, The Atlanta Journal-Constitution. We take the field on many Sundays. The PA systems play "The Star-Spangled Banner" to start the games. Jay and I add an abbreviated rendition of "O Canada...we stand on guard for thee," our nod to the recent expansion of major league baseball to Toronto and Montreal.

Jay yells, "Un, Deux, Trois!" and we're underway.

Our bond strengthens until it encompasses wives, children, my aging parents, careers, illness and recovery, and more recently, the birth of my first grandchild—all the curveballs that life throws at us. We share our kids' experiences, mark life cycle events together. When the time comes to write college essays, Jay reviews my kids' applications and those of the other kids in the neighborhood with the rigor and scrupulous honesty of a Jesuit.

This is who he is.

Tony Cameron, a standout pitcher on Pepperdine's powerhouse mid-1970s baseball teams, and the son of Hollywood idol Rod Cameron also crosses my path. More than a decade after he hung up his cleats, Cameron makes an appearance at a North Atlanta Men's Senior Baseball playoff game against my team. The day we meet I'm batting leadoff for the Mustangs. An Atlanta sportscaster named Chuck Dowdle is pitching. We're down 1–0 in the third inning, when their manager Kevin Barnes, calls "Time." He marches out to the mound and signals with his left hand, "Give me the lefty."

Tony is fiercely competitive and proud. He's still borderline pro material, and here's Barnes, this Atlanta Hawks statistician, waving him on because there are runners on first and second and he doesn't want the game "to get out of hand." This is the third inning. Cameron is rolling his eyes. He can still throw a fastball close to 90 mph. Coach V, from the third base coach's box could see what was unfolding.

I step in. Cameron throws a heater right by me.

"Strike one!"

I'm shaking in my boots. In my head, I hear Valentine saying, "Protect yourself at all times."

Cameron's nostrils are flaring, a bull about to gore a matador. He fires. I swing, and barely tip it.

"Strike two!" the umpire shouts.

Cameron asks the umpire for a new ball. Valentine knows that only a pro would do that.

To counter, I step out of the batters box, take a deep breath and look down at Valentine. He knows I'm way overmatched and he gives me the bunt sign.

With two strikes, I lay down an "immaculate" bunt. It's hugging the foul line, hits a pebble, and stays fair. Cameron, a lefty, instinctively bounces off the mound to field the bunt, but slips on the wet grass, and falls on his ass. His competitive nature and athletic ability is such that he fires the ball toward first base, the first baseman misses it, and the ball goes into right field. Both runs score, and I'm standing on second like the cat that just ate the canary. Cameron, steaming, keeps turning toward me. He mouths, "F..k you! F..k you!"

He goes on to strike out nine batters and wins the game. As I'm packing up my gear, I look up. Cameron is standing in front of me. He smiles and says "Hey you gutsy SOB, lets grab lunch some time." And just like that, the beginning of a beautiful friendship. I later learn that Cameron and Killebrew were about to play in a much a higher level semi-pro league and they'd decided to play a few games in my league to get their arms in shape. Funny how things happen sometimes.

Dr. Mark Brenner and I hanging out with Joe Namath at Mickey Mantle's restaurant Central Park South, 1994.

In the years ahead, we'll go on road trips together to Cooperstown, Yankee Stadium, Camden Yards, Fenway Park, MLB Allstar games at Jacobs Field in Cleveland, Coors Field in Colorado, AT&T Park in San Francisco —sometimes in the off-season where Tony's connections and my "no such thing as a wrong turn" stubbornness propel us inside the gates, once onto the base paths of Doubleday Field in Cooperstown where we're running and sliding and stealing home plate like Jackie Robinson and Ty Cobb. The field is covered in snow but we do it anyway, simultaneously sliding into home plate.

We travel to Big Sur and Carmel, Pebble Beach and the Napa Valley vineyards with our wives. He calls me "hermanito," little brother, and Tony becomes the big brother I never had. What I remember most about him is his toughness and absolute loyalty. In these years, Elisa is working as a loan officer for First Georgia Bank in Atlanta, still a rare thing for a woman in the South. She's thick-skinned but as you'll see, there's a limit. One day after work, Tony swings by our new house--we're in the process of finishing a kitchen--and finds Elisa in tears. Seems our contractor, a big gruff guy with a short fuse, has gone bananas, cursing, screaming, even threatening her. Tony

Cameron somehow tracks down the address of the man's office and, unbeknownst to us, pays the guy a visit. Tony is about six foot three and his pitching weight in college was 210 pounds. Tony waits and waits, and finally he corners the guy. I'll leave the rest to your imagination. When Elisa arrives at work the next morning, she finds a written apology and a bouquet of roses at her desk.

When you become Tony's friend, he's got your back.

This is who he is.

Of course, the catalyst in all this is Coach Valentine. If you're visualizing the Gipper in baseball spikes, think again. Coach is overweight, unkempt, an omnivore who'll eat six hot dogs and your whole pizza if you turn your back. Other than baseball, he has the attention span of a flea. He's diabetic, seemingly always on the verge of anaphylactic shock. He has Vietnam stuff going on in his head and weapons—an evil set of sharpened awls among them—stashed in his car. I'm a middle-class kid from New Jersey. You don't want to be on his wrong side, but I never doubt he'll die for me. He's rumored to have a mysterious Vietnamese wife—he speaks fluent Vietnamese!—no one has ever seen. He sets batting practice to music—he's light on his feet!—and can waltz the "Blue Danube" while gliding right and left in the batter's box—and smacking the shit out of baseballs.

On the road, his personal habits are such that none of the veterans will room with him, except for me—what they called in Vietnam the FNG, which stands for "f..king new guy" who must deal with the most dangerous stuff because he's new. One morning, I stumble into our bathroom and find him scraping clumps of fungus off his bloody toes—his foot is next to my toothbrush. Another time, we're sharing a duplex room; I'm on the top level. Deep in the night, I hear what sounds like tinny Hawaiian music. I step out to the railing and look down. Valentine, stretched out on the carpet, flashlight and transistor radio by his ear, has set up a base camp on the living room floor.

There are a thousand stories out there about Coach McDonald Valentine Jr.—war stories, baseball stories, madcap adventures, and stories of lives he influenced and undoubtedly saved. Many of them are true. You tend to think outsized lives like Coach Valentine's go on forever, but they rarely do. In the early 2000s, his long-uncontrolled diabetes began to destroy the blood vessels supplying his heart, brain, kidneys, and other vital organs. He spent the last months of his life an amputee, wheelchair-bound in a VA hospital near Emory University. "Undaunted" sounds like a cliché, but in Coach's case it was true. When Jay Smith and I visited him, our Mustang ball caps firmly on our heads, Coach was in great spirits. He introduced us all around as "his boys." I was proud to hear him say that. And he'd put his Ranger reconnaissance skills to good use, figuring precisely the time and location where the warm freshly made chocolate chip cookies were served on each floor of the facility. He went charging from one elevator to another, the two of us in tow.

Coach died June 11, 2009, and was laid to rest in the National Cemetery in Canton, Georgia. Over the years, he'd told us he wanted Gene Autry's recording of "Happy Trails" played at his funeral. Sure enough, there's a beat-up Victrola atop the chapel's altar. A few dozen of us—many former military—are there to say farewell. Among them, my friend Stash's son, Michael Kalish, to whom Coach Valentine had taught baseball and life lessons that put him on the road to success. Michael, an internationally known artist, flew in from California to deliver a eulogy. He says he's passing Coach's legacy to his 11-year-old son and it comes down to one sentence: "Coach Valentine taught boys how to be men, and men how to be boys."

I confess the scratchy music brought tears to my eyes.

144

Chapter 14

I don't see my friend Rabbi Arnold Goodman as some kind of conduit to God. He's a real person.

In Paterson, New Jersey, it was Temple Emanuel for the high holidays, to prep for my bar mitzvah, and for life cycle events—weddings and the occasional funeral of a big macher; all told, a few times a year. When I arrive in Atlanta, Elisa and her family are members of Ahavath Achim (A.A.), a synagogue run for a half-century by a learned, respected—some say feared—rabbi named Harry H. Epstein. Born early in the 20th century in Lithuania, Epstein, the scion of a long line of rabbis, held a PhD, a law degree, and numerous other religious and academic accolades. Stiff and formal—he never moved away from the podium during a sermon—he was legendary for disciplining parents and unruly children in the middle of a service. Not exactly a magnet for me. When Rabbi Epstein retires, A.A.—like most southern institutions conservative in outlook—surprises me by seemingly hiring his polar opposite, Arnold Goodman, a tall, gangly lawyer from Minnesota.

The "Sandak": Rabbi Arnold Goodman occupies the seat of honor in Acre, Israel, November 2019.

Both men are intellectuals, but Rabbi Goodman also proves himself open-minded and compassionate, a spellbinding orator. A fierce egalitarian, he encourages women to read the weekly Torah portion, to seek positions of authority in the synagogue, to attend rabbinical school—wise in both spiritual and worldly matters. Thus far, my dealings with the Jewish community essentially involve softball and tennis, but I find myself showing up to hear Goodman's sermons—not just for Jewish opinion, but also for his learned and well-thought-out arguments on every issue. I remember him holding forth on the dismantling of the Berlin Wall, the near-miraculous story of Nelson Mandela, Ronald Reagan's adopting Martin Luther King Day as a national holiday, the ascents of Sandra Day O'Connor and astronaut Sally Ride, and Brooklyn's

Bobby Fischer's world-stopping upset of Boris Spassky in the Cold War of chess.

Away from the pulpit, Goodman maintains a certain professional distance, understandable given what I suspect are his liberal, progressive politics and the determination of many of A.A.'s old-guard families to oppose any whiff of change, a battle that continues to this day, three rabbis later. His compassion, wisdom, and generosity burst forth when Elisa and I confront the debilitating stress, exhaustion, and occasional despair of years of infertility and the unimaginable loss of our premature twins. My father, ever the Marine, tells me, "I'm sure you'll make the right decision." Rabbi Goodman is there for us, at the hospital, talking to me by phone every day for weeks, gently guiding me through psychic shoals where Sheldon Ezor can never go. Thirteen years later, Goodman is at my side when our son Zachary makes his bar mitzvah—my father grumbles about missing one of his beloved Nets home games to fly to Atlanta, but, of course, he does.

By the end of the century, Ahavath Achim is facing a diaspora of young families—the lifeblood of any synagogue—moving into the Atlanta suburbs. Suddenly, youth is in demand. In his early seventies, Rabbi Goodman is named senior rabbinic scholar and fulfills his dream of making "Aliyah" in Jerusalem, where he remains to this day. Replacing Rabbi Goodman is easier said than done. Several interim rabbis pass through A.A. before Neil Sandler is named senior rabbi in 2004. My friendship with Goodman grows deeper with time and distance. In his eighties, he'd happily board a jetliner in Tel Aviv, fly to Atlanta or Boston, where he has family, even catch an Uber to get around. Over the last few years, he and I establish a ritual: When he's in Atlanta fulfilling his scholar-in-residence duties, I pick him up and we head over to General Muir in Druid Hills—our new favorite deli—for a schmear. The lectures this man delivers at the synagogue are sharp, well-argued, not to be missed. "He's still got it," members of the congregation whisper. It took a pandemic to interrupt these annual trips.

He's seen so much, dealt with so many people, and is so willing to share his knowledge. How blessed I am to have such a friend and mentor in my life. Rae, his beloved wife, passed away a few years ago. Now in his nineties, he lives alone in his Jerusalem apartment, his everyday needs looked after by his dutiful son Ari and daughter-in-law. He's hardly a shut-away.

In November 2019, I travel to Israel as part of an outreach to young Jewish men sponsored by the Jewish Federation of Greater Atlanta. I wasn't young, but my biking buddy Mark Silberman is Federation president and he creates a last-minute spot for me. A week later, I realize we're being hosted by the Israeli Defense Force—think Aliyah Meets Top Gun—so we jockey F-16 flight simulators, drive ATVs through the desert, blast away with semiautomatic weapons. I have some free time so I call Rabbi Goodman. We meet for lunch near my Jerusalem hotel. At one point, he mentions he'll be traveling north to attend a bris on Sunday, the offspring as I discover to my delight, the result of a comingling of Sephardic and Tunisian Jewish families.

Bobby (front row, second from left) attending a day of flight training at "The Squadron" in Ramat HaSharon, Israel. Bicycle buddy and past president of Atlanta Jewish Federation Mark Silberman stuck me in his suitcase and took me on a most memorable trip.

"We've got room for one in the compact car," he tells me, waggling the invite, "but it's gonna be a long drive."

Sound familiar?

"Count me in!"

I arrive at the Rabbi's apartment Sunday morning. "Abba (father)," Ari shouts. "We gotta go!"

"My friend Bobby from Atlanta just arrived. He's coming with us."

"Good." Ari says this with the casual gruffness so typical of Israelis, so I'm not sure if I'm welcome or resented.

We head downstairs, squeeze into a cramped Asian econo-box, stow the baby seats, make a quick stop to collect the rabbi's sister-in-law, and we're off; west out of Jerusalem, north along the coastal highway, past Haifa, and a couple hours later, into Acre. I don't know what I'm expecting, most likely bunkers or desert huts, but everything is crisp, clean, white; low-rise apartment buildings intersected by smooth roads and aesthetically designed green space. Acre itself is a walled city dating back to the Phoenicians (1500 to 300 B.C.), rebuilt during the Crusades, then part of the Ottoman Empire, and now modern-day Israel. En route, I'm treated to an archetypal family road trip encompassing history, geography, gossip, and an unexpected exchange of political barbs between the conservative Ari and his more liberal-leaning father and maternal aunt, all delivered rapid-fire in Hebrew and English.

Enjoying a meal in Jerusalem with my Rabbi and friend Arnold Goodman, November 3, 2019.

A sumptuous feast awaits us, as over-the-top as any Jewish or Italian wedding in New Jersey or Brooklyn, only here many of the delicacies are exotic to me. One spread features eight different chicken liver dishes including chicken liver with candied dates and chicken liver wellington; savory skewers of lamb, ground beef, and chicken; couscous; pickled lemons; rice-stuffed peppers; burekas; and dozens of Middle Eastern desserts. Food, folk dancing, reedy Middle Eastern music, a capella singing—people bursting into song and others joining in—and a gigantic hora that seemingly goes on forever.

In acknowledgment of his age and learning, Rabbi Goodman is honored as the sandek ("companion of the child"). He sits on a throne at the front of the hall. When the moment comes, a long-bearded rabbi dressed in black garb lays the child (atop a pillow) on a table to Goodman's right. The father approaches, lifts the child on the pillow, and gently places it in Goodman's lap. The mohel dressed in white approaches. In a few seconds the deed is done, and the celebration continues.

At some point, Rabbi Goodman, whose life has now been entwined with mine for 30 years, calls me to his side. "Bobby, I'm the sandek," he says with a twinkle in his eye. "This is the blessing of all blessings." And then he blesses me and our friendship.

In Hebrew, blessing means "to bring down Divine abundance."

And that's what his friendship has given me.

All quiet on the Western Wall overlooking the Old City of Jerusalem, November 2, 2019.

BOBBY EZOR | ORDINARY LIFE IS EXTRAORDINARY

152

Chapter 15

"They lead us over back roads to a dank underground storehouse, the stuff of tourist nightmares. We return with a truffle the size of a coconut."

Agrigento, Sicily. We're driving southeast of the Valle dei Templi (Valley of the Temples), a wonder of the ancient world dating back to a Greek colony founded in Sicily in 500 B.C., but it's the roadside sign, Punta Bianca, small, hand-painted, and barely noticeable that catches my eye.

"What's that?" I ask.

"White Point," says David Levinson, translating.

"Let's go see."

David and his wife, Debbie, our travel companions, are literally "Mr. and Mrs. Italy." They've made 50 trips, raised their children, written books.

The four of us—David, Debbie, Elisa, and I—turn off the paved road, the conventional and predictable path, and soon are bumping our way along a narrow sandy track dotted with flowers and dwarf palms. After maybe 20 minutes, the road ends. We park the car and start walking. And walk some more. I'm beginning to think this might be an actual wrong turn when suddenly the sky opens and I'm blinded by the light. We find ourselves on a cliff of the purest white and seemingly made of chalk. The Mediterranean sparkles below, its turquoise water shading into green and deeper purples. The "White Point" lettered on the sign refers to the Punta Bianca Natural Reserve. We climb down the cliffside, eroded over eons into a staircase, giddy with excitement. We arrive at the stone ruins of an abandoned carcere, a jail, literally a few yards from the surf. We have a hunk of watermelon and a bottle of wine—no corkscrew—so we decide to await the sunset. The afternoon lengthens, and the wine, the friendship, the sun, and the spectacular setting make for a priceless moment that remains completely alive and resonant.

To think that if I hadn't noticed that sign, hadn't made that turn, hadn't seen it through. That's the point of this book: There are few wrong turns in life; if you are lucky, there are only unexpected opportunities for new experiences and new friendships. There's another tale I'd like to share: my lifelong love affair with Italy, with Italian people who seem to live con brio wherever you find them, who strut and fret like the world is a stage and they are star players who live out loud. I love Italian food, Italian cinema, Italian cars, Italian wines, Italian women. In short, Italian passion.

Like any hot-blooded Italian male, I fall madly in love with my father's best friend's wife. Lee Leoni Bey is voluptuous, gorgeous, and seductive; a Sofia Loren lookalike, though at age six I couldn't tell Sofia Loren from a Yankee Doodle. I never sleep with Lee Leoni, but I fall asleep with her widowed mother—another classic character from Italian folklore—who dresses in black and sleeps in a dark room under a crucifix, an eye-opener for a Jewish boy. Lee Leoni teaches me how to fold a slice of hot pizza before popping it into my mouth and the succulent joys of lobster. Unlike the crustaceans boiled into rubber by New England Yankees, Lee Leoni's aragosta is prepared fra diavolo in a spicy tomato sauce sautéed with garlic, basil, oregano, and chiles.

Looking back, I got my first taste of Italian at a handful of Paterson restaurants—Scordato's, Steve's, Johnny and Hanges, and Pizza Town USA on busy Route 46—loud, rambunctious red sauce palaces whose owners and regular customers, I now realize, could have been *The Sopranos*. My father and I gorge guilt-free on veal parmigiana, spaghetti and meatballs, and baked clams. Shellfish and veal parm are dishes my kosher Grandma Sadie will not allow in our house.

1965. Eastside High School.

When I start high school, Paterson is sliding into a long decline. Factories are shutting down; white flight is gutting neighborhoods; poverty and crime are on the rise; a trickle of immigrants—Hispanic, Caribbean, African, Palestinian, Bangla Deshi—that will eventually become a wave. I'm mostly oblivious—secure in my white middle-class cocoon. There are Jews and Protestants and Irish and Blacks among my classmates and on the faculty, but many of my strongest high school memories involve Italians. One involves Vivian Paruta, a social studies teacher.

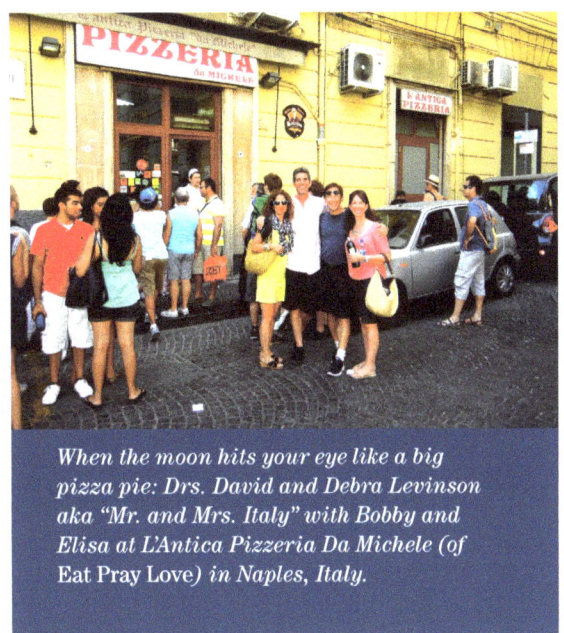

When the moon hits your eye like a big pizza pie: Drs. David and Debra Levinson aka "Mr. and Mrs. Italy" with Bobby and Elisa at L'Antica Pizzeria Da Michele (of Eat Pray Love) in Naples, Italy.

On the day in question, a Black student named Walter Ferguson is sitting, sulking in the cafeteria. Mrs. Paruta approaches and says something—maybe the wrong thing. He doesn't respond. She keeps after him and I can see he's about to blow. She reaches for his ear as if she's going to pull it. Walter jumps to his feet and smacks her right across the face. Deathly silence descends on the cafeteria. She staggers back. I can see Ferguson's handprint on her cheek. Seething, he sits back down. I see Walter Ferguson's life pass in front of me—troubled Black teen assaults teacher, arrested, drops out of school, convicted of assault, sent to the notorious Garden State Youth Correctional Facility, branded forever as a violent offender.

But it doesn't happen this way. A minute later, two men rush in. They grab Walter by his arms and begin to escort him out of the cafeteria. They're security guards, or maybe custodians. Suddenly, Mrs. Paruta darts over and talks to them.

"Walter and I will work this out," she says. "OK with you Walter?"

The kid has tears in his eyes and nods. "Yes," he mutters. "I'm sorry." The two of them leave together. The next day, Walter is fine.

They don't show this side of Italians on *The Sopranos*. Mrs. Paruta could have ruined him—many teachers would have—but she chose understanding and compassion, making an impression on me that I feel to this day. Then there's that man of constant sorrows, Buddy Eanelli, the brilliant and doomed jazz pianist who tours with Peggy Lee, Mel Torme, and Gene Krupa, and winds up leading our Eastside Ghosts high school marching band. And Amelia Nardella, prom queen. Sweet, smart, beautiful, and way out of my league. If high school was Italian opera, I'd be the character forever chasing the unattainable, especially after Amelia scribbles in my yearbook, "Don't ever forget me, because I won't forget you."

Needless to say, I still have that autograph a half-century later.

Atlanta 1973 to 2020.

A gifted photographer and graduate of the Rhode Island School of Design, Chip Simone is one of the seminal friendships I make when I move to Atlanta in 1973. Growing up working class in Worchester, Massachusetts, Chip battles an abusive father and the "curse of low expectations" that has sidetracked so many talented individuals. Given his furious dedication to the purity of his vison, I often think Chip would have been at home in the Renaissance; just ask his wife and muse Kathy Egan. He lives an ascetic life, but Chip learned to hone his craft through discipline and determination. He can also make a great pizza.

This intoxication with gathering, preparing, and eating great food is another trait I share with Italians, compared with the American notion that "food is fuel." A filmmaker friend of mine was scouting in Italy with director Oliver Stone. By chance, they encounter the great Marcello Mastroianni walking down the street. Stone is ecstatic to meet one of his idols and begins talking. And talking. Finally, Mastroianni politely breaks off the encounter.

There are rewards for taking the road less traveled! Mio amore Elisa and I at remote Punta Bianca, Valle Dei Templi, Sicily.

"Why are you going?" asks Stone, at the time one of the most famous directors in the world.

"I must go cook pasta," says Mastroianni.

Through Chip, I meet Vince Coppola, my coauthor, another working-class Italian who propelled himself from the banks of Brooklyn's polluted Gowanus Canal and the grip of wise-guy culture to graduate from the Columbia University School of Journalism and win a job at *Newsweek*. Vince has written six well-received books, but like me, he's happiest in the kitchen preparing a meal to share with friends. Through Vince, I meet Joe Cavallo, a former Green Beret and FBI agent. While working in Miami Beach during the 1972 Republican National Convention, Joe used his downtime to prepare tomato sauce, which is sacramental to him. The scent wafted through the floors of the hotel and up to Richard Nixon's suite. Meanwhile, Attorney General Richard Kleindienst smells the sauce; he investigates, he tastes, he raves. ("The old man would love this!" he says.)

Years ago, David Levinson and I played basketball together at the Atlanta Jewish Community Center. For some reason, we drift apart for 20 years. Life happens—we live in different parts of Atlanta, our kids go to different schools. We travel in different circles. In 2008, Debbie hears through the grapevine that Elisa and I are thinking about biking in Italy. She calls Elisa.

"We really love Italy!" Elisa says.

"Bet you don't love Italy the way we love Italy," Debbie says with a laugh.

Next thing I know, we're biking through Tuscany, and visiting Florence, Cortona, Montepulciano, a half-dozen of those jewel-box cities that have fired the imaginations and passions of travelers for a thousand years. And the food... On other trips, we visit Puglia on the heel of the boot, the fabulous Amalfi Coast, and of course, Sicily, which to me encompasses all of Italy's warmth and charm.

What I discover is that there are other people out there who, if you make a wrong turn, are willing to see it through. The friendship flourishes because we do things the average traveler wouldn't do. In Tuscany, traveling with David and Debbie's son, Jacob, we learn Sting is performing at the Teatro Verdi in Florence. Of course, it's sold out. We don't even blink. Next thing I know we're in the Queen's Box staring eye level at Sting. When a truffle-hunting trip flops, Debbie and I travel at night with two shady-looking characters who speak no English. They lead us over back roads to a dank underground storehouse, the stuff of tourist nightmares.

But we return with a truffle the size of a coconut.

The Feast of Saint Joseph (March 19) is one of my favorite Italian holidays. By tradition, the friends and family of anyone named Joseph are obliged to present a box of pastry—typically, Zeppole di San Giuseppe prepared once a year—to the saint's namesake. Joseph Cavallo, a Sicilian, cooks a gigantic feast for his Georgia friends. One of his showcase dishes is pasta con le sarde, an unlikely sounding but delicious Sicilian dish made with bucatini pasta, sardines, golden raisins, fennel, pignoli, and bread crumbs. Joe has a farm north of Atlanta where he cooks for 20 to 40 close friends including many from law enforcement. Elisa and I, David and Debbie, and Vince and Suzanne are among the guests.

Two years later, it's my turn. A lawyer from New Jersey with a lifelong love of all things Italian hosts the fabled San Giuseppe feast in Georgia unlikely as that sounds. Cavallo, Vince, Lou Arcangeli, and David and Debbie Levinson help prepare the food. David is not only a skilled chiropractor, but also a first-rate pizzaiolo. Dean Martin shows up, at least a reasonable facsimile of Dean. Chip Simone, Nikon in hand, documents the occasion. Dozens of my friends, many of whom you meet in this book, are there. Wine flows. Storytellers tell stories, some of them true. No doubt to be told and embellished over the years. Family, friends, love, food—my whole universe in a nutshell. I couldn't be happier.

BOBBY EZOR | ORDINARY LIFE IS EXTRAORDINARY

162

Chapter 16

"May I call you Bobby?"

NBA Hall of Famer Jerry West

June

1987. I ease the gold Rolls Royce into the parking lot of the Forum in Inglewood. I get out, preen for a nonexistent scrum of photographers, and hand the keys to Wes Matthews, my one and only client in an unlikely venture into sports agentry. I could not have picked a more auspicious moment: The NBA finals are about to get underway. Pat Riley's Lakers—Magic Johnson, Kareem Abdul-Jabbar, James Worthy...and Wes Matthews—vs. K.C. Jones' Celtics Larry Bird, Kevin McHale, Robert Parish, Danny Ainge. Wes's smile is bright enough to light up the Forum, as is his compulsion to create never-ending mischief. He grabs the keys and disappears. When he comes back, two young women—not Halle Berry or Courtney Cox either—all tight spandex and bulging boobs are hanging out of the car.

"My man, Eaz! (as Wes has christened me), "Say hey to my new friends." Next thing, we've arrived at Nicky Blair's, one of the hottest spots on Sunset Boulevard that caters to A-listers like Sinatra, Stallone, Denzel, and Clint. In the 1980s, the Lakers are the hottest thing in town, so the throngs of stars and stargazers recognize Wes Matthews as Magic Johnson's backup. The two women are as gracious and polite as can be, but they don't fit the sleek Lakers/Hollywood image. When the check arrives, one of them winks at me: "Wes got us a couple tickets for the game. We're gonna get all dolled up!" Looking back, I should have paid closer attention.

The next day, I show up at the Forum to pick up my own tickets. I have some housekeeping to do for Matthews, but this is basically a courtesy call. Talk about life's unexpected turns: Somehow a chance meeting in Atlanta with an unheralded ballplayer from the University of Wisconsin has landed me, a personal injury attorney, in Jerry West's office. "May I call you Bobby?" Jerry asks the first time we meet. ("Yes, you may, Jerry," I imagine answering.) As a kid, NBA basketball was the holy trinity to me: Wilt Chamberlain, Oscar Robinson, and Jerry West. West, a 14-time All-Star and 1972 MVP is a demigod, the Mantle of basketball. In 1987, Jerry is in the final quarter of an astonishing 40-year run as a Lakers player, scout, coach, and now, general manager. His teams will win five NBA titles between 1982 and 2000, including this year's matchup against the Celtics.

Wes Matthews will pinball through a half-dozen NBA teams, seven Continental League clubs, a chaotic personal life, and a truly catastrophic stint in Milan, Italy. Yet, there's something likable, even magnetic about Wes that even "Riles" (Coach Pat Riley) cannot resist. Magic Johnson thinks he's charmed. In 1979, while playing for the Wisconsin Badgers, Matthews scored 30-odd points and lofted an astonishing half-court shot in the final second to defeat Johnson's Michigan State Spartans 83–81, a stunner that Magic never forgot. Wes is a savvy ball handler, a masterful field general, and a serious student of the athletes who play the game at the highest levels. He knows the moves, the feints, the dinks, the dribbles, the little giveaways of every guard in the NBA. He can mimic them precisely and this makes him invaluable to his teammates, including Magic Johnson. From the bench, he's a cheerleader, jumping and waving his towel at the end of the bench; a joker; a fun-loving, good-hearted, wild and crazy guy. He can't understand the odds are stacked against him, that he's destined to suffer the indignities of 10-day contracts—one mistake, one missed layup, a jump shot that rims the basket and he's gone. And there are 10 guys eager to take his place. This year, he's fit and eager to contribute, but Magic is indefatigable and nearly indestructible, a virtuoso who plays every minute of every game as if he's conducting a Beethoven symphony.

Something is wrong. The alarm that registers on Jerry West's secretary's face the moment I walk into the front office should have made that clear. "You may want to come by another time," she says carefully. The warning goes right over my head, intoxicated as I am with the notion of dropping in on Jerry.

"He's pretty stressed out."

"How bad can things be?"

(He's playing for the NBA championship, right?)

"Whatever Jerry says, please don't answer him!"

Walking in there is like walking into a hurricane. West is yelling the moment I step through the door. "Over my f..king dead body will this f..king prick be back next year!...Nobody does what he did! It's unthinkable!" I have no idea what the man is talking about, but with Matthews it could be anything. I'm like one of those dopey TV weathermen standing in a flooded street daring the hurricane to blow them away. Jerry is literally apoplectic, a full-blown Jekyll and Hyde transformation.

"Nobody has ever done anything...!"

It occurs to me: This guy can kill me if he wants to.

The screaming subsides into shouting and I surmise Wes Matthews, literally a flea on the ass of the Lakers organization, has done something way beyond the pale. Turns out he walked those two

Patience, Tolerance, and Persistence: Lakers GM Jerry West and I agree to resign Wes Mathews, June 1987.

"flamboyant" young women into the Forum Club where the politicians, the big wigs, the Hollywood moguls—Jack Nicholson, Dyan Cannon, Larry David, Leonardo Di Caprio, Sly Stallone, Steven Spielberg, Sharon Stone—the crème de la crème of the moneyed season ticket holders congregate.

Jerry thinks Wes had the balls to bring a couple of crack whores into the inner sanctum. No doubt he does, but it's not true! Jerry has no idea they're really nice girls. I don't say a word other than, "Good luck tonight," as I slip out the door.

The series will be remembered as one of the great matchups between Larry Byrd and Magic Johnson. The Lakers win the championship 4–2. Johnson is named MVP. At some point, I have to fly back out to LA to take a meeting with Jerry West, a prospect I'm now dreading. To my utter surprise, West says, "This is against my better judgment, but Riles likes your boy. So we're going to give Wes one more contract."

The Lakers repeat the next year. Matthews is cut, but he leaves with bonus money and two NBA Championship rings in his pocket. I'm gifted Wes's championship hats, signed by each Lakers player, a pretty good deal.

This agent thing opens my eyes. I never make any money to speak of, but I learn a lot of stuff from the inside. I attend seminars; I meet coaches, players, managers, agents, wives, and baby mommas—and hear some things I'd rather not hear. Whether it's baseball, football, or basketball, journeyman players are little more than livestock. To this day, I believe that if one NBA coach or GM had taken an interest in Wes as a human being, paid him a decent wage, allowed him to mature as a player, lessened the financial pressure, and all the other pressures on him, he'd have blossomed—never a Magic, but possibly a Mo Cheeks. Instead, the philosophy was "Keep him hungry." Not just Wes, but a hundred guys like Wes. I listen as legendary coach Cotton Fitzsimmons compares his players to horses. "You gotta know when to pull 'em out," he says. I saw him yank Artis Gilmore who'd made a mistake and stick him on the end of the bench. Cotton let the seven foot two, 240-pound center sit there seething until he decided the steam was just right. "Okay, Gilmore, get in there!" Artis charged off the bench like a bucking bronco and kicked the shit out of the other guys.

An African American who grew up without a father figure in the Black section of Bridgeport, Connecticut, Wes really didn't have anybody looking out for him. For the longest time, he couldn't look out for anyone, including himself.

Two years later, my phone shrills in the middle of the night. My son Zachary is snug in his crib so more than likely it's Wes Matthews.

"What now?" Elisa groans.

At this point, with the assistance of my friend and associate attorney Ken Behrman, I've successfully navigated Matthews through "deadbeat dad" claims—his son is current Milwaukee Bucks standout Wesley Matthews Jr.—and a handful of warrants typically sworn out by unhappy paramours. I've taken over his finances, kept him up-to-date on his financial obligations, even managed to sock away some money for him. But simply put, Wes is wearing out his NBA welcome. Competitiveness and ferocious play do not make up for an erratic shot and erratic behavior.

This year, he's playing for Ranger Varese in the Italian Basketball Federation, which limits the number of foreign players on the roster of each team. He's joined other former NBA players like Rick Mahorn, Joe Barry Carroll, and Reggie Theus. Matthews is actually en route to becoming a superstar in Italy. The money is good and I've just negotiated a million-dollar shoe deal for him. He's on the front cover of the federation's All-Star program. Of course, he can't speak Italian and the isolation and cultural differences inevitably take a toll. (Bill Bradley, the Rhodes Scholar, future Knicks forward, and U. S. Senator, suffered a similar disconnect when he played in Italy in the mid-1960s. Matthews is no Bradley.) The Italians have an expression, *sputare sangue*, which means "to spit blood," i.e., a player who leaves his heart on the court. Apparently, Wes takes the expression literally: He responds to a particularly egregious call by spitting in the ref's face.

A gift from my client Wes Mathews: Lakers Championship cap signed by all the players.

"They've thrown me off the team!" he shouts over the phone. "Thrown me out of the league...thrown me out of the country! We're going to sue the shit out of them!" There's more to the story. To this day, Italians treat Black ballplayers shamefully. The referee apparently responded to Wes's outrage with a racial slur, perhaps *tissone* (a chunk of charcoal or burnt wood) or *melanzane* (eggplant). Matthews didn't need to understand the language to get the meaning. Needless to say, there's no lawsuit and the shoe deal goes up in smoke.

I've been Wes's agent for five years. And I still worry that he might not show up for a meeting, a negotiation, a hearing. The two of us are now part of a dysfunctional family unit that includes Elisa, Pammy (Wesley Junior's mother), Wes's mother, a string of his homeboys in Bridgeport, numerous girlfriends in various NBA cities, former coaches, various representatives of law enforcement and the judiciary, and inevitably, determined debt collectors. After vowing he's settled down for the umpteenth time, Wes will inevitably plead the inner-city equivalent of the Fifth Amendment. We've confided in each other, entertained each other—he attends my daughter's bat mitzvah and plays gentle basketball with my son Zachary who calls him Uncle Wes. When my first grandchild is born in the summer of 2020, Wes sends a congratulatory note: "... give Sam the Man a big uncle welcome!"

I'm invited to the soul food picnics he throws for his Bridgeport posse. I've written a screenplay about him—*Dream*—but ultimately, we never become best friends. This bothers me because I know Wes has the biggest heart. When I ponder this, Wes is a free throw that rolls around and around the rim, but inevitably drops away. We're on a lifelong roller-coaster ride—(forget business)—dizzying to look back on, heart-stopping, and way too stressful. Besides, I have a family of my own to raise.

Of course, we stay in touch. A decade ago, his son, Little Wes, is a standout guard at Marquette University. Pammy, with whom I'd built a friendship riding herd on Wes to keep up his child support payments, tells me she worries her son has the skills, but not the ferocity to make it in the NBA. She wants Wes—time heals all wounds—to teach his six-foot-five son the "in-your-face" aspects of the game. A font of aggression on the court, Wes is eager to reconnect with his boy. At the time, the problem is Wes can't show his face in Atlanta. There's an outstanding warrant for his arrest. The specifics are less important, but a jilted girlfriend used the legal system to accuse him of a crime—nothing sexual or larcenous or violent—a familiar pattern in the old Wes's life. Once again, I'm drawn in. I work the case and the charges are dropped in a judge's chambers on Christmas Eve. The African American woman—dressed in business attire—winds up happily singing carols with the middle-age Anglo judge. I discover standing there uncertainly that Eartha Kitt's "Santa Baby" is their favorite song.

Father and son unite. Wes does his magic. Undrafted, Wes Jr. is a walk-on. Jerry Sloan likes what he sees and gives him a one-year contract with Utah. He'll eventually sign a $30 million NBA contract.

A few years ago, I learn Wes is back in Bridgeport, living a very modest life and looking after his aging mother. It happens that Elisa and I have to be in nearby Stamford for a life cycle event.

"Wanna go see Wes?" I ask.

Of course she does. Next thing I know, we're driving through the neighborhood where he grew up. There's the court with the chain-link nets where Wes launched himself into a schoolboy legend a half-century ago.

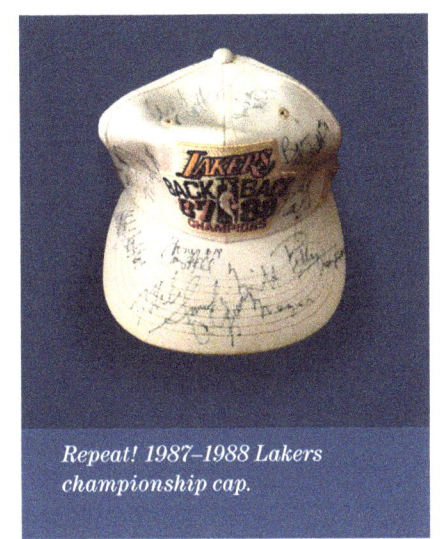

Repeat! 1987–1988 Lakers championship cap.

"I think that's his house," I tell Elisa.

A big Black guy stares at me from the sidewalk. I nod politely at him.

"Bobby?"

"Yeah?"

"Bobby!"

Wow, I attended a picnic a good 30 years ago. This man remembers me. Wes and his friends would hold these reunions in the parks along the Pequonnock River. Nothing or nobody fancy. Just these guys who played sports, none of whom made it big time, getting together, laughing and joking and teasing like they're still in high school. I feel a twinge of nostalgia, or more likely jealousy. This is a world that is forever closed to me.

"Is Wes here?"

The man nods his head.

"Eaz!"

A 60-year-old Wes Matthews comes flying out the front door.

"Lady E!"

He throws Elisa in the air and swings her around like he's done a hundred times. We catch up. His son is enjoying the long-term NBA fame and stability Wes could never grab on to. Wes is coaching the girls' squad at Greenwich Academy, an elite prep school, and hoping for a shot at a pro-berth that may never come. "The basketball gods have allowed me to give back what I learned from some of the greatest basketball minds," he tells a suitably impressed local reporter. "It's my duty to pass on that knowledge." Strange as it sounds, he seems at peace.

Pop-up visit to Bridgeport, Connecticut. Elisa, Wes Matthews, and me. Still crazy (though a bit more mellow) after all these years, January 26, 2019.

There's a practice in a few hours. I drop off Elisa in Stamford and return to watch Coach Matthews at work. He's patient, observant, and thorough. And exuberant: The same court general he was in the NBA.

"Before I go, I wanna see your mom." This meeting has become unexpectedly poignant for me.

"Eaz, she really ain't seeing people. She doesn't come out much in public."

"Go back up there. She doesn't have to do anything. Tell her I just wanna say, 'Hey.'"

Wes turns around and skips back upstairs. The truth is, his mother loves me because she knows I always had Wes's best interests in mind. It sounds simple, but try to forge such a bond in a world where sharks and con men run wild. I sent her little gifts and knick-knacks to let her know I was thinking about her. One Christmas, I sent what generously might be called a "bejeweled" picture frame.

She still has the frame. It's sitting on the mantelpiece...empty.

"How come there's no picture?" I ask when we walk into the living room.

"I just love the frame!"

Wes and Elisa take pictures. I later have them printed, sized, and mounted. The frame she's had all these years now has a picture in it—of Elisa and her, Wes and me.

All of us.

174

Chapter 17

Uncle Bobby Meets Frankie No: "No matter how old they get, they become the second-graders they were when they first met.

For a weekend, my dad is a kid again."

Zoe Kessler, daughter of otolaryngology surgeon Scott Kessler

Since

the 1970s, Rao's, a near-mythical Italian eatery in East Harlem has been the absolute toughest seat in New York City. If you call and are fortunate enough to get a human being on the line—mostly no one answers—you are brusquely told to try again in a couple months or "maybe next year." There are no reservations, just table assignments that were designated decades ago by co-owner Frank Pellegrino and his aunt, Anna Pellegrino, who was married to Vincent Rao sometime in the last century. Some designees come weekly, others monthly, some maybe only at Christmas. When one of these "owners" passes away, the table is often inherited by their heirs. Diners can arrive when they like, the table is guaranteed for the evening. However, they can "give" the table to family members or friends for the evening, a system that sounds as inbred as Appalachia.

What is it you don't understand about the word "No"?

Just to get through the door, an outsider like me has to know "somebody who knows somebody." That's how Pellegrino, who sits outside, guarding his domain like some red sauce Cerberus, earned his nickname "Frankie No." Of course, the food is supposed to be revelatory, and on any given night, you might see Scorsese, DiCaprio, Woody Allen, Keith Richards, Billy Joel, Rudy Giuliani, Gloria Estefan, even Bill and Hillary. Bo Dietl (a louder-than-life ex-NYPD detective who was a regular on the Don Imus show) commands an outsized table. And, of course, some guys whose names you don't want to know are usually huddled at the bar.

Peacoat Brigade: Scott Kessler and Bobby, circa 1976.

I've been traveling to NYC regularly since I moved south in 1973. My parents and sister are still living in New Jersey, my best childhood buddies, Danny Lawrence and Scott Kessler, are an Uber ride away from the Newark airport. My daughter Danielle and son Zack attend college in the Northeast; Elisa and I will pop up for a play, a party, a new restaurant, an exhibit, and, of course, a Yankees playoff game.

This weekend, I'm staying with one of my closest friends, Dr. Scott Kessler, and his family in their rambling Upper West Side apartment. I've known Scotty since elementary school. The two of us prepped for our bar mitzvahs together in Hebrew school. I was the sports nut, obsessed with Mantle and the Bronx Bombers; Scotty, academically and artistically brilliant, worked on science projects and entered art contests. I went to the University of Maryland because if Scotty, my most brilliant friend, was going there, it had to be a great school, right? We'd drive back and forth to Jersey together, and have these deep, thoughtful conversations that have stayed with me to this day.

Today, Scotty is one of the most highly regarded otolaryngology (Ear, Nose & Throat) surgeons in the country with a stable of high-profile, demanding patients including Madonna, Mariah Carey, Mick Jagger, and Andreas Bocelli. The Scotty I've come to see is the kid who'd forever joke, giggle, sing, and make mischief with me. Head and neck surgery is precise, exacting, and exceedingly delicate. For decades, Scotty has worked under unimaginable pressure. His wife Debbie ("Mom"), whom I've grown to love, and teenage children worry that he rarely takes a break or a vacation.

This is a cue for "Uncle Bobby" to make a needed appearance. "My dad tends to be a bit stubborn and unwilling to go out and do things," his daughter Zoe writes. "However when Bobby comes, it's like his vacation away from reality, even if he's not relaxing. Bobby is always able to talk him into doing some crazy thing, because Bobby's answer is always, 'Why not?'"

"No, no, no. Well, if you insist, Uncle Bobby." Scott Kessler, circa 1976.

"Why not?" I plead with the grim-looking guy with the gravelly voice when I crash Rao's that afternoon.

"You gotta own a table," he repeats as if "owning" a table to eat in a restaurant in a city with 25,000 other restaurants is the most obvious thing in the world.

"Come back in six months."

"Here, take my card," I plead, pulling it out of my wallet. "Call me if there's a cancellation." This approach, sweetened by a cash incentive, has served me well in Barcelona, Firenze, Manilla, Beijing, the capitals of the world, but apparently not at

Three Musketeers: Dr. Scott Kessler, "Uncle Bobby," and Brad Jacowitz.

a nondescript corner dive in East Harlem. It doesn't help my case that I'm wearing tennis whites—a long story—right down to the wristbands, which probably makes me in the eyes of the Italians, a real jadrool (loser).

"No way I'm calling you back."

Then I learn that tonight the legendary jazz trumpeter Hugh Masekela is being honored at the Apollo Theater as part of a concert series, *Sounds of Freedom: From South Africa to Harlem*. In 1968, Masekela's impossibly catchy "Grazing in the Grass" became the background music of every New Yorker's life. Poet Maya Angelou will also be on hand. No way can Scotty and I miss this opportunity, and besides, the landmark 125th Street venue is just a few crime-infested and broken glass-strewn streets from what is now the holy grail, Rao's.

My niece Zoe picks up the story: "After half-an-hour arguing, Bobby finally gets my dad to agree to go. When they leave for the Apollo, Dad is overly nervous and uncomfortable. The show is sold out and started half an hour ago."

Turns out the Apollo is a piece of cake. I'd already snagged three tickets—Scotty, Brad Jacobowitz, and I—in the nosebleed section of the balcony. It's a very small world: Brad, who manages the portfolio of an eastern European billionaire, is Irwin Deutsch's nephew and a Yankees fanatic. We've become kindred spirits. Once inside, I work my magic and soon we're sitting in the orchestra, a dozen rows back from the stage, drinking signature martinis. The concert is fabulous, even historic, but now, it's Rao's time. I've gone full Italian: Armani pullover and sports jacket, Bruno Magli shoes, Borsalino hat. I leave Scott, also dressed in black, and Brad outside, and stroll nonchalantly through the front door.

Frankie No spots me from across the room and heads over. I'm standing at the crowded bar next to a very large guy, his friends, and three gorgeous young women jabbering away like Lisa Simpson in shrill, nasal shrieks. At first, Frankie No doesn't recognize me, then comes a glimmer of recognition, "the jadrool in the tennis shorts" who won't take "no" for an answer.

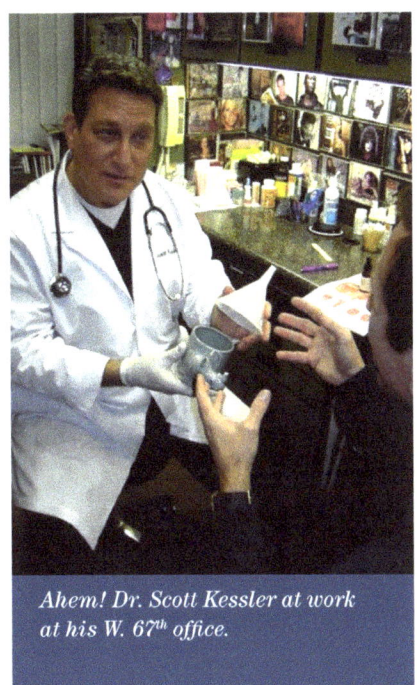

Ahem! Dr. Scott Kessler at work at his W. 67th office.

"I told you there was no table! You gotta leave."

"Can't a guy even get a drink in this f..kin' place!" I blurt.

Turns out, that's the right thing to say.

By now, this feels personal. I have no idea that Frankie No has sent hundreds, maybe thousands, of guys just like me slinking out the door in what must look like a march of shame to the folks stuffing themselves with outsized meatballs, veal parm, lemon chicken, stuffed clams. "I can't eat, so I don't exist." He actually refused to seat Warren Buffet. I also don't know that six months before a local wise guy, Louie "Lump Lump" Barone, shot Albert Circelli, a mafia-made man to death after Circelli rudely

Friends forever: Scott and Bobby enjoy a few quality moments at the William Vale Hotel in downtown Brooklyn, June 2018.

interrupted Broadway actress Rena Strober midway through her impromptu rendition of Barbra Streisand's *Funny Girl* classic, "Don't Rain on My Parade."

"I lost face," Barone told the cops who arrested him. "I had to defend my honor. I had no choice but to shoot him. No choice but to kill him." Not the best way to frame your defense in a murder trial. The truth is, Rao's has been a wise-guy destination since Lucky Luciano ate there before being deported to Italy before World War II. John Gotti, the infamous "Dapper Don," was a customer. It's part of the appeal.

"Dere a problem heah?" This from the big guy at the bar.

"This guy…" Frankie No begins.

"What's the problem?" the big guy asks. I tell my story. "I flew all the way up from Atlanta. My best friends are waiting outside. We've been trying to eat at Rao's for years."

"Yada yada," as Jerry Seinfeld might say.

"Yous heah dat?" the big guy shouts to his companions at the crowded bar. "All the ways from Atlanta!"

"No shit!" they shout. Even "Nicky Vests," the bartender known for his fashion statements, joins in. "Whadda you drinking?"

"Martini. I gotta get my friends."

"Go get 'em," the big guys says. He turns to Frankie, "Dese guys are wit me."

Scotty and Brad come piling in. For the next two hours, we stand at the bar as drinks miraculously appear in front of us. The big guy gets diners at the dozen or so tables—he seems to know everyone—to deliver us choice morsels of their meals. Every now and then, someone gets up and sings along with the hits playing on the jukebox—Sinatra is a favorite—and everyone joins in. By the end of the night, even Frankie No is grinning. He hands us gift bags containing jars of Rao's pasta sauce and packages of signature pasta. No check ever appears. Thanks, Big Guy, whoever you are. It's great but a bit weird, like we're freaks ("All the ways from Atlanta!") and at the same time, welcome at least for one evening.

Kessler family: Zoe, Scott, and Debbie at son Max's wedding, June 2018.

To me, the Rao's experience was like a raucous wedding or bar mitzvah, only you can get killed. In the next few years, I discover Rao's outposts have sprung up in Caesar's Palace in Vegas and in Hollywood—yes, the lines were crazy long—but the experience never as much fun as in the Bronx.

Scotty and I stagger home giggling, half-drunk and reeking of garlic. As Zoe puts it: "As usual and without a doubt, Uncle Bobby had pushed my dad to his limits once again. Without having realized it, my dad got his vacation away from reality that

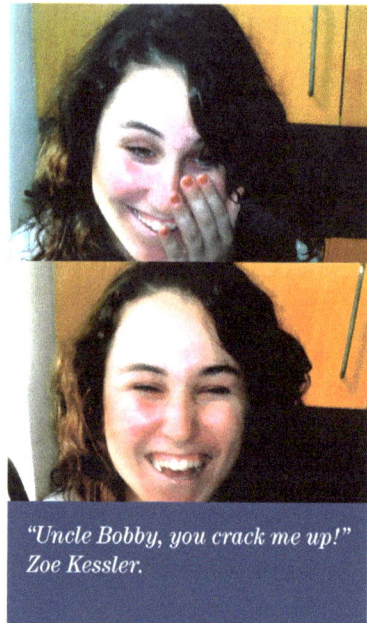

"Uncle Bobby, you crack me up!"
Zoe Kessler.

night. No matter how much it seems my dad needs Bobby, Bobby needs my dad just as much. The uncle I know never lets a day go by without living it to its fullest. Why waste one day when you only have one life to live. The friends you make when you're young become more important as years pass."

She's right. Nothing has really changed. Not at the deepest level, even now as two guys who ran around together in elementary school are themselves grandfathers.

Chapter 18

"Lookin' for adventure and whatever comes our way…"

Steppenwolf, "Born To Be Wild"

In 1962, the Copacabana is NYC nightlife. I tag along with my parents—Sheldon schmears the headwaiter—and there I am, a big-eyed 12-year-old under a canopy of fake palm trees, surrounded by voluptuous Copa girls, watching Sammy Davis Jr., Steve & Eydie, Shecky Greene, and Dean Martin & Jerry Lewis. Wise guys lurk in the background like sharks. Cigarette girls dressed like sexy tropical fruit wriggle by.

1992.

Save The Robots is the hottest club in NYC. The Copa is gone, glittery theater district giving way to Lower East Side grunge. The cigarette girls are now flamboyant transvestites in wigs and ballgowns. Among them, "Lady Bunny," a former Atlantan and sidekick of the soon-to-be-famous drag queen RuPaul. Hard drugs, cocaine, ecstasy, poppers, and heroin are everywhere, speeding the fentanyl explosion of the next decade.

"Ya Talkin' To Me?"

The first wisps of onrushing development and gentrification that will transform East Side tenements and the industrial warehouses of the West Side into tourist-friendly "attractions" are in the air.

I'm up for the weekend, along with my buddy Tony Cameron (the rock-steady, hot-tempered pitcher), Dr. Scott Kessler (my boyhood friend), and Brad Jacobowitz (who joined us for our Rao's adventure). Other than the fact we're mostly married and inching toward middle age, we're—as Steppenwolf puts it—"looking for adventure"—though not "whatever comes our way."

Scott is wired into the ongoing club scene. A night out, he tells me, doesn't even begin until the wee hours and runs 'til the sun comes up. It's hedonistic far beyond the "free love" hippie era, traces of which persist like psychedelic cave drawings in the East Village. At 3:00 a.m., we arrive at Robots, a nondescript storefront on Avenue B in still-notorious Alphabet City. It's a madhouse; a seething, multihued mob of club kids, celebrities, skinheads, punks, frat boys, trustafarians, transvestites, and Andy Warhol wannabees, all striving for the attention of the gatekeepers, some of whom, like Craig Ferguson (Robots), Mark Benecke (Studio 54), and Haoui Montaug (Danceteria) come to possess godlike power over ordinary mortals.

Tony Cameron, who looks like a golf pro, is instantly ignored. Brad takes a shot and is turned away. Dressed in my Borsalino and Italian finery, I size up the situation, cross the street, and climb the steps of a stoop in front of a tenement. Now, head and shoulders above the hapless proletarians, I watch as the bouncer, a big white guy, picks and chooses—thumbs up or down—like Caligula deciding who lives or dies in the Colosseum. We make eye contact. I wait a beat, then hold up four fingers.

"Come ahead," he motions.

I have no idea what the man assumes, but I gather my crew.

"We ain't getting in there," Tony grumbles.

To this day, he's amazed that I pulled this off.

We stumble into a wall of throbbing sounds, driving techno beats, a mad crush of sweating, stoned people, a full-blown rave. I'd been to Woodstock; this experience is visceral, overpowering, dystopian in the way watching *Planet of the Apes* first affects you. What really strikes me is the line dance, like at a fraternity party, and people going down the line strutting their stuff, except these people are out of this world. I recall one woman amid the barrage of outrageous input, wearing a see-through plastic dress and carrying a see-through purse. She strolls through the line, and later I see her in tears, methodically taking things out of the pocketbook and putting them back in.

"What are you doing?" one of us asks.

"Searching for my sanity."

5:00 a.m. in the Westside Meatpacking District.

By the 1980s, "meatpacking" in the string of faded commercial butchers and warehouses on 10th Avenue had taken on new meaning: the late-night trysting place of choice for thousands of gay men, male prostitutes, and transsexuals. Hellfire, one of the early gay sex clubs in the district, defined the scene—wide open, anything goes, Dionysian, as if these long-repressed men are determined to make up for lost time. AIDS, which would kill more than 100,000 New Yorkers, exploded out of the meatpacking scene.

The reluctant photographer: Scott Kessler dining in the city with yours truly.

When we arrive, Hellfire has sealed its infamous glory holes, supposedly cut back unhealthy behaviors, and has begun to attract a sliver of straight and celebrity voyeurs. Think Studio 54 without borders. No alcohol is served, a nod to a NYC liquor license that I imagine is not forthcoming in a torture chamber make-believe or not. Hellfire has rebranded itself as The Vault, hardly reassuring to me. Honestly, if not for Tony Cameron as my bodyguard I never would have gone in.

Inevitably, we split up and go our separate ways. Eyes wide shut, I find myself in an alcove where a shirtless guy is draped over a Harley-Davidson. He's handcuffed to the handlebars. An S&M queen in full regalia is gently flogging him with a cat o' nine tails. I look over and a tiny Asian man in a tuxedo and patent leather slippers—he reminds me of Kim Jong-un—is masturbating while watching the spectacle. Next to him is a massive guy, think Odd Job in Ian Fleming's *Goldfinger*. The S&M queen now has a lighted candle and is dripping molten wax onto the shirtless guy's back.

"Oh...oh...oh," he moans in pain, or maybe pleasure.

"I can't believe this is going on," I say mostly to myself. Odd Job hears this and steps toward me. Our eyes lock—I'm in imminent danger—and then I'm whisked away.

"You're going to get your f..king self killed!" Tony hisses.

The next scenario in this culture of cruelty and self-abasement features an overweight girl on a swing suspended over a bar. The men and women at the bar touch and fondle her over their orange juices and Virgin Marys like the female vampires in *Dracula*. Next there's this tough-looking, hairy-chested guy in a lace tutu with breath so bad it'll knock you down. He has chains around his neck and arms that connect to his penis. His member has a bell attached, which he rings.

"What are you into?" Brad asks.

"Humiliation," he says.

"You win," I say.

Later, I wonder about the joke. It's funny in the moment, but not funny. The odds are this man—many of these men—didn't survive the AIDS era. And I wonder about the impulses or experiences that lead a fellow human—ridiculous seeming or not—to crave humiliation and shame. To hang from a swing and expose one's innermost insecurities for the world to see and touch. Is it nature or nurture that forces them to act? Shamelessness or its first cousin, loneliness? I'm older now and sometimes I wonder about that sliver of a vanishing world we glimpsed as the sun was rising over the Empire State Building. At the moment, there are cabs to catch and tales to tell.

Part of the club scene is the morning-after brunch. We cab over to a place—I think it was on Greenwich Avenue—where scores of club denizens are drinking Bloody Marys and looking much the worse for wear. After bacon and eggs and Western omelets, the four of us—this band of brothers—cab back uptown and sleep the day away at Scott's house.

Searching for our sanity: Studio 54, mid-1980s.

BOBBY EZOR | ORDINARY LIFE IS EXTRAORDINARY

Chapter 19

None of my friends or anyone we knew remained in Paterson.

Everyone left, except for my father. Paterson was Sheldon's town.

PASSAIC FALLS AND CHASM BRIDGE, PATERSON, N. J.

GREETINGS FROM PATERSON N.J.

Main Street, Paterson, N. J.

BATHING BEACH AT BARBOUR'S POND, PATERSON, N. J.

Main Street at Market, Paterson, N. J.

All roads lead to Paterson, New Jersey.

Father's Day Weekend 2019.

When I leave for college in the summer of 1969, my hometown of Paterson, like so many once-vibrant northeastern industrial cities, is in precipitous decline. Paterson, where Alexander Hamilton's vision of the newborn United States as a manufacturing power, bursts forth at the Great Falls on the banks of the Passaic River in northern New Jersey. The Silicon Valley of the 19th century, Paterson attracted venture capitalists, engineers, inventors, artisans, and entrepreneurs, among them Peter Colt whose descendant Samuel invented the pistol known to millions of western fans as the "six shooter." Thomas Edison designed one of the world's first hydroelectric plants at the falls. Paterson's foundries produced the first steam locomotives. America's silk industry—think sails for the famed Yankee Clippers—began as a start-up in Paterson.

My dad Sheldon D. Ezor (16 years old) in Paterson, autumn 1940.

In his way, businessman Sheldon Ezor, my father, embodies this tradition. The grandson of impoverished Eastern European immigrants, he was born, raised, and laid the foundation for his later success in Paterson—vision, hard work, and iron discipline. His first job in a downtown shoe store hondling women's accessories ended in disappointment, but he stayed madly in love with the place for the rest of his life. Downtown burned in the aftermath of the 1968 race riots; violent crime soared; white flight and "block-busting" by greedy realtors took their toll. The school system collapsed. Our street went from affluent white to working-class Black. None of my friends or anyone we knew remained in Paterson. Everyone left, except for my father. Paterson was HIS town. He'd take Elisa and me for rides through the downtown: I'd see broken bottles and discarded hypodermic needles; he saw silver-coated memories of Mandy Berg's deli and an idealized childhood.

After a very full life, Sheldon Ezor passed away on December 30, 2015. He was 91. On Father's Day weekend, Elisa and I fly to New Jersey for his unveiling, in the Jewish tradition, the formal dedication of his tombstone symbolized by the removal of a veil, cloth, or handkerchief draped over the stone. We arrive a day early and we spend that mild spring day walking around Paterson. To my surprise, a wave of bittersweet memories (you've read about them in earlier chapters) flood over me: My father describing how the young Lou Costello of Abbott and Costello fame would bounce him on his knee in front of my grandparents' luncheonette, not far from the falls.

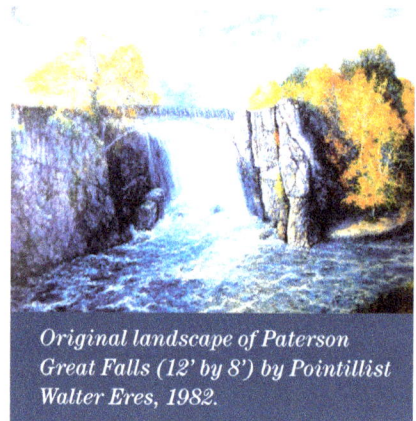

Original landscape of Paterson Great Falls (12' by 8') by Pointillist Walter Eres, 1982.

In those days, young Sheldon's neighbors on Graham Avenue included the Taub family, founders of ADP; Frank X. Graves, future four-time mayor of Paterson; Frank Lautenberg, later U.S. Senator; and Larry Doby, the first African American ballplayer in the American League and future Hall of Famer. Sheldon would one day co-chair the Paterson Alumni Association Bicentennial and serve as president of his synagogue and as chairman of Barnert Memorial Hospital.

My old Eastside Park neighborhood with its stately houses is being reborn; gentrified is too strong a word, but urban pioneers, including teachers and a subset of gays—always a telltale sign of urban renewal—are buying the big houses on the cheap, sprucing them up, planting flowers in the front yards. Hinchcliffe Stadium, where I marched behind Buddy Eanelli in the Eastside Ghosts marching band, is being renovated.

We're smiling by the time we head downtown. Here, we encounter another unexpected change: Main Street, Market Street, Grove Street, the old commercial heart of Paterson, have somehow been transformed into a sprawling Middle Eastern bazaar—hole-in-the-wall restaurants, pharmacies, import-export businesses, halal butchers, hookah lounges, cafes, music stores, mosques, newsstands. Nothing fancy, but definitely alive and vibrant, the sidewalks crowded with families and children. I'd read that Islamic terrorist cells had operated in the area before September 11, and my Jersey friends have warned us away, but we spend a delightful afternoon strolling in and out of shops, noshing and dining at two simple, but delightful restaurants, Al Basha and Aleppo, both on Main Street. Down the block, Fattal's, a Syrian bakery offering an astonishing array of savory delights—I'm reminded of Jerusalem, or Balducci's in Manhattan—provides the pastries we serve our guests who attend my father's unveiling.

Artist Walter Eres with friend and fellow artist Barbara Hemphill, Mill Street in Paterson, June 15, 2019.

From the downtown, it's a 15-minute walk to the Great Falls, a spectacular waterfall carved by receding glaciers 13,000 years ago. Two centuries ago, Alexander Hamilton saw the falls as an engine of industrial power. In the 20th century, like much of Paterson, the falls plunged into decline, a place to avoid given crime, pollution, human blight. A stereotype, to the point that *The Sopranos* showcased the graffiti-clad rocks as the likely setting for a gangland execution.

Hesh to victim: "You wanna go for a walk in the rocks?"

In 2011, the wheels turned again, thanks largely to the efforts of John Lawrence and Leonard Zax, two Patersonians committed to giving back to their hometown; the falls were officially designated a national park—think Yellowstone and the Great Smoky Mountains—and a cleanup got underway. Given my father's love for Paterson,

I'm thinking of making a donation in his name, maybe symbolized by a memorial bench, bronze plaque, or some other artifact facing the cascading water. I can see it in my mind's eye: "Sheldon Ezor, A Great Patersonian." I'm strolling around the falls when I notice a man making his way unsteadily up the embankment. In his seventies, he's clearly struggling. I extend my arm and pull him up the last few steps.

Generations of Ezor Memories: Bobby visits the Great Falls, Paterson, New Jersey, June 15, 2019.

Odd, how fate or destiny enters your life. Of course, I strike up a conversation. Bearded and dressed in loose-fitting, paint-stained clothes, the guy is no vagrant, but an artist, an Austrian named Walter Eres. He tells me he's lived around the falls for 50 years, most recently in Essex Mills, an industrial loft converted to studios and artists' residences. In turn, I tell him about my father and his devotion to Paterson. After a while, Walter's girlfriend, also an artist, shows up and then Elisa, who I know is thinking, "Here's Bobby's latest best friend!"

Walter invites us to his studio, its walls covered with unframed oils in the style of Jean Baptist-Simeon Chardin. Dominating it all is an enormous oil painting in the pointillist style of 19th-century French artist Georges Seurat. Of course, it's of the Great Falls. The impulse hits me: "Buy it and they will come," i.e., donate this monumental artwork in Sheldon's memory. The fact that Seurat, Walter Eres, and Sheldon Ezor are all born on the same day—December 2—seems more than coincidence.

But that's not what's going through my mind. I'm thinking about the many times my father and I had visited the falls, when he told me he'd jump into the pond at the foot of the falls, a thing I'd never done. I'm thinking that I'm so proud of my dad—you now know we didn't always agree—for having stuck with Paterson when everyone else left. How proud he'd be to see his city finally rebounding, though it will be a long road and the work will be done by other waves of immigrants. It strikes me that the future Paterson will look nothing like the city of my privileged childhood, or that of young Sheldon, a boy who came of age without a father who spent his whole life determined to prove himself.

And maybe that's a good thing, an American thing.

BOBBY EZOR | ORDINARY LIFE IS EXTRAORDINARY

Chapter 20

Sometimes, I wish I could take my helmet off and just throw it away. Wish I could get rid of these clips. Wish I could be 12 years old with no helmet and my U.S. Keds on my feet and my best friend beside me.

Tour de Robért

David Levinson and Bobby aka Duvid and Bocce biking in Lecce, Italy. Bocce, Duvid, and Luigi (Dr. Louis Okun), in Senoia, Georgia. Bocce, Duvid, and Luigi in Palmetto, Georgia. Bobby reuniting with boyhood friend Dr. Richard (Richie) Levine.

Our Atlanta peloton. Bocce in Lecce, Italy. Mark and Linda Silberman escort me up the Ashcroft Climb in Aspen, Colorado.

Pearl Pass Road in Aspen. Bobby and fellow riders on Mr. and Mrs. Italy's Heel of the Boot ride through Puglia, Italy. Bocce and Luigi riding the horse farms of Palmetto. Recovering from rotator cuff surgery with empathetic fellow warrior Tony Cameron.

More

than a half-century ago, Danny Lawrence and I wheeled our heavy Schwinn bikes down the Broadway hill and, grinning like 12-year-olds, headed out on the highway. Like the generation who came of age between the Depression and World War II, our parents were overprotective, but oblivious to what mischief could take root in the minds of boys raised free of the shadow of hunger and turmoil. Korea was receding in the rearview mirror; Vietnam a decade away. Like "a true nature's child," we were "lookin' for adventure"—maybe not the heavy metal thunder of the next decades, among the placid lakes and still forests of Tallman, New York, 26 miles north in Rockland County. I now realize it wasn't the destination driving us, but the journey, the bond, the friendship that melded two sweet suburban boys into an unspoken but fierce connection still palpable a lifetime later.

In my mind, it's always a bright summer morning. I feel the breeze rippling my hair, the sun warming my face, the tingle of danger that is part of any adventure. My hunger for new experiences, new places, and new people is beginning to take root, an appetite still unfulfilled. With maturity comes the realization that friendship is more than the sum of memories and mutual experiences occasionally revisited. It's alive, in the moment, at our fingertips. A repository of our earliest dreams, hopes, joys, and passions. A deep well should we choose to drink from it. Too few of us do, caught up as we are in the humdrum routines and distractions of daily existence. I've been blessed with more than my fair share of friendships.

Cautious and reliable—as he'll be his whole life—Danny is a few bike lengths out-front riding point. He's mapped every pothole, noted the busy intersections and heavily trafficked roads to keep us safe, a living GPS system. As for me, I have a peanut butter and jelly sandwich and an apple in my saddlebag.

Who could have imagined that a centuries-old, muscle-powered machine would be the vehicle that delivered me to the future? As a boy, I'd imagined Ferraris, Chevy Chaparrals, flying cars, atomic shoes, anti-gravity machines. And yet, over the handlebars of my bicycle, I glimpse satisfaction, fulfillment, even serenity as I begin the final laps of my existence.

A glimmer, but I hope my heroes Mickey Mantle and Muhammad Ali and Jerry Garcia were as fortunate. Arriving at enlightenment seems complicated, but it isn't. For much of my life, I've been ultracompetitive athletically, whether as a tennis player, a basketball player, a softball player, or a semipro baseball player. I saw each of these games as a transition to the next. And in my late fifties, I return to biking, this time on ultralight bikes with skinny tires. Sure my strength and endurance has declined, but, given my success with Coach Valentine on the baseball diamond, no amount of time, expense, or surgery (rotator cuff, 3; knee, 2) was going to dissuade me. Thanks to my friend and orthopedic surgeon Steve Wertheim, who did the repairs and made me good as new.

And yet, after a year or so, I'm not a happy biker.

The solution, ironically enough, comes from my internist, Dr. Alan Bleich. At the conclusion of my annual physical, we always wind up in the room containing "the big green machine," his very antiquated treadmill. I'd be hooked up to the electrodes and the test would start. On the wall is a poster of a solitary jogger facing miles and miles of rolling hills. The caption reads, "The victory is not always to the swift, but to those who keep going."

Making conversation, as he looks at the EKG printout, Dr. Bleich asks me, "Anything new?"

"Yeah, I've been riding with this group of people and when I get up to the top of a hill, these guys aren't winded, but I really am. Huffing and puffing. Is there something wrong with me?" (To make matters worse, group leader "Eddie" would rib me: "Why are you breathing so hard?" Some other riders don't find "Eddie's" manner amusing and never ride with us again.) A few days later, Dr. Bleich sends me my results in the mail. "All in all, you are doing great..." the letter reads. "P.S. With reference to your inquiry, you're hanging out with the wrong crowd."

He was right. Getting mixed up with the wrong crowd, the very thing my father warned me about when I was 13. This time, a gang of middle-age affluent day-trippers determined to "get their exercise in" and rush back to their lives. In the beginning, I enjoyed the competition. After a few months riding a 22.5-mile route known as the "Buckhead Bellyache," I was consistently topping the hill with the first three or four of the dozen or so men and women on the ride. Wonderful, if you think gasping for breath while staring at pavement for two hours is your connection to nature. For this bunch, it was flaunting their impressive skills, toned bodies, crazy expensive gear. Never, "Let's take the sunnier, shadier, or more beautiful route." Always, "I have to be back early, I've got the Georgia Tech game, or I'm having my hair blown out."

What a long strange trip it's been: My first wheels, 1955.

I did have enjoyable conversations and some good times. Particularly with Ruthie Rosenberg who'd break into Steppenwolf's "Born to be Wild" every time we'd hit the start of a long rolling downhill. And with Mark Silberman, who led the men-only trip to Israel to hang out with macho Israel Defense Force guys—another unexpected left turn I was happy to take. And with Lenny Silverstein, who traveled the world sailing in international regattas like Ted Turner.

Inevitably, coming off a joyless Sunday morning ride, I get so distracted staring at my odometer trying to squeeze in the last few yards and see it tick 40 miles, I miss a speed bump in a church parking lot and go flying over the handlebars. I tear my rotator cuff (again). It takes me many months of rehab to get back in the saddle.

And then I start riding with David and Luigi.

Everything goes from black-and-white to technicolor.

Autumn 2020.

I'm riding across a landscape of gently rolling hills, southwest of Hartsfield International Airport. Horse farms and residential communities—some, like Serenbe, planned to the nth degree—have sprung up around Tyrone and Palmetto and Union City, towns most Georgians have never heard of. Runaway development, the leading edge of Atlanta's urban hurricane to the north, has displaced the old truck farms and dairies, but to an outsider, the country roads, the herds of lowing cattle, and the organic smell of manure might as well be Italy. The Sunday morning air is crisp and clean. White-washed country churches, doors open in welcome and parking lots full, dot the country roads like fields of mushrooms. Grass glistens in the morning light; tiny spring-fed waterfalls sparkle and gush. In a month, wispy smoke from wood-burning fireplaces will perfume the morning air with the smell of frying bacon and biscuits. The Schwinn Corvette of my youth has given way to an ultralight Trek Domane with a super slick electronic shifter, a nod to the intervening half-century of wear and tear on my knees. I'm dressed, truth be told, like one of the Mighty Morphin Power Rangers my kids used to watch back in the 1990s.

Bracketing me are two other Jersey natives, David Levinson and Louis (Luigi) Okun, biking buddies who've become dear friends. You might have met David happily tossing handmade pizzas in my kitchen on St. Joseph's Day or watching his son Isaac kayak down a roaring Tennessee mountain gorge. On our bike rides, childlike, he'll happily follow anything—a bird, a butterfly, a hippie girl seemingly out of place in the 21st century dancing in a waterfall on her birthday. Like David, Luigi came south to attend chiropractic school and stayed. These many years later, despite his Jersey accent and his colorful biking gear, the locals know him and his wife Lori as "regular folk."

Together, my two friends are loving husbands and fathers, manly men, tough as nails, and yet heartbreakingly generous and sensitive. Like me, and so many other men, I suspect they trail an unspoken history of pain and loss, but push past it like the tenth stage of the Tour de France.

Luigi has one of the sweetest hearts. Eight years ago, the three of us and our wives, Elisa, Debbie, and Lori, traveled to Italy together. The triple crown of my favorite things—food, friends, and adventure. One night, we're driving at dusk in Tuscany when a driver in another car hits a dog in the road. Luigi sees it happen. He pulls over and gets out. He takes his coat and wraps it around the injured dog. He stays with it until word spreads and its owner appears and rushes over. The man, who speaks no English, takes in the scene. He holds and comforts his beloved dog—it's absolutely heartwrenching—and then he hugs Luigi in the street like they're lifelong friends. In that moment, they were.

We all were.

My long-ago bike rides with Danny Lawrence were adventures, everything that followed goes right back to that first taste of freedom. Freedom. I can still feel it on these Sunday mornings. We're out here. Nobody is bothering us. We don't have any deadlines. The world and its mad distractions retreat like April snow in the sun. We stop and go as we please, as fast or as slow as we want. Head for the same country store run by the same ol' boy week after week and buy an apple that tastes very much like the apple I packed in my Schwinn saddlebags when I was 12. We stop at Super Mercado La Bendicion (The Blessing) where the food is savory, hot, and cheap, but the real blessing is how much these simple, honest, hardworking people contribute to this magical world.

On our last ride, Louie and I talked about the 2020 Tour de France, won, as it turned out, by a 22-year-old Slovenian riding for the United Arab Emirates. Louie and I are in our sixties. And it struck me that, I too, am coming to an end. My bike-riding adventures like my tennis and hardball games, will pass. Already, we're planning to cut our rides back a notch and just enjoy the pure pleasure of the ride and the nature, the camaraderie, and the view. I need the exercise, but what I crave is the fun of being out there, relaxed and enjoying every minute. After all, how long am I gonna be here?

Sometimes, it all feels like a dream. I take off my helmet and throw it away. I have no clips on my pedals. And I'm 12 years old again with my U.S. Keds on my feet and my best friend Danny beside me.

BOBBY EZOR | ORDINARY LIFE IS EXTRAORDINARY

211

BOBBY EZOR | ORDINARY LIFE IS EXTRAORDINARY

212

Epilogue

"A Lovely Bunch of Guys"

Keith Richards

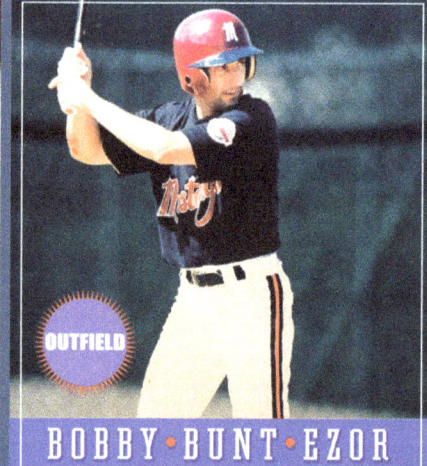

A lifetime ago, I found myself in a hotel room in Cabo San Lucas at 3:00 a.m. I'd flown from New York to Paris, then to London, on to Barbados, then across the continent to Los Angeles, and finally to the Baja Peninsula in Mexico. Sitting across from me was Keith Richards, yes, that Keith Richards. Curled sinuously around a sofa was Patty Hansen, Keith's blonde supermodel wife.

On a month-long assignment for *Newsweek*, my job was to hang out with the Rolling Stones when they were not on tour, to see and hear and feel what their lives were all about. Mick Jagger had just turned 40 and was making noise about leaving the band for Hollywood, to design men's fashion, write books, maybe all three. He told me in that languid cockney accent he affects, "Rock and roll has become B-pitchers." When I mention this to Keith, he grins and shrugs off Mick's whining. He says his goal is to keep playing, to die "in harness" like his Mississippi Delta idols, Howlin' Wolf, Muddy Waters, Robert Johnson. I ask Richards how Jagger—cofounder of the "world's greatest rock and roll band"—can possibly be bored.

"Mick," he says, "is a lovely bunch of guys."

I never forgot that quote. Early in 2020, as the Covid pandemic was beginning its onslaught, my friend Bobby Ezor asked if I'd work with him on his memoir, though he never used that term. It was more like "I have a few stories I'd like to tell." I've known Bobby for 20 years. When his widowed mother Estelle was slipping into the long night of dementia, Bobby painstakingly re-created her New Jersey apartment in an Atlanta nursing home.

I also knew Bobby as an attorney, a sports nut, a food aficionado, the mensch who allowed my son, an Iraq War veteran, to live rent-free for a year in his Buckhead condo; a guy who moved mountains to see that I'd survive a devastating cancer. Thanks to Bobby, the chairman of the head and neck department at Mt. Sinai Hospital in Manhattan operated on me. When rounds of chemotherapy and radiation left me shivering uncontrollably, Bobby showed up with a thick (and stylish) woolen blanket. When I couldn't bear to eat, he brought me New Orleans-style bread pudding that somehow he'd tracked down in Georgia. He did these and other mitzvahs in what I now realize is classic Bobby style—all out. Once you are Bobby's friend (whether you appreciate, deserve, or abuse this marvelous gift), he makes you feel you are the most important thing in his life. I'm convinced this is one of the reasons he and Elisa are still crazy in love.

In 2015, he and I volunteered to put together a documentary on the 125th anniversary of Ahavath Achim, his Atlanta synagogue, though how a guy from New Jersey wound up with that assignment was beyond me. Now I know the answer: Bobby saw a need and ran with it, a defining pattern in his life. Our film wasn't a poorly shot and clumsily edited assemblage of droning grey beards and whining children. No way. Bobby convinced Tovah Feldshuh, who'd just come off her record-breaking run of *Golda's Balcony* on Broadway, to come to Georgia and narrate the film.

I've been a working journalist for more than 40 years. I've been approached many times by people who say they have "a great story to tell," and they rarely do. Bobby never says that. He believes ordinary life is extraordinary...that there are no wrong turns...that friendship, commitment, and compassion are signposts on the road to fulfillment, and maybe, transcendence. In Bobby's world, adventure (or misadventure) always lies around the next turn, over the next hill, and he is forever open to it. This can be an exhausting way to live; it seems so much easier to stand back and let the world go by.

Bobby Ezor never stands back. Researching this book, I began to realize I was hardly alone. There are dozens, probably hundreds of others—friends, colleagues, teammates, and no doubt, total strangers—to whom Bobby extended his hand, his expertise, his time, his bad jokes, and his heart. As with millions of boys in the 1950s, Mickey Mantle was Bobby's idol for reasons now obvious and complex; even the seemingly most well-adjusted kid can be achingly lonely. Here, Bobby burst through the third wall. He went from ordinary to extraordinary. He hung out with Mantle.

The Mick tongue-kissed Elisa! In another adventure, the two of them snuck into Muhammad Ali's Atlanta hotel room and found themselves observing the Champ in a moment of utmost compassion. It wasn't about the orange slices.

And so, we confront the question at the heart of every human story. Who is this guy?

Keith Richards had it right.

Bobby Ezor is a lovely bunch of guys. And I'm blessed to know him

Vincent Coppola, February 2021

About the Authors Plus*

Vincent Coppola is an award-winning journalist who has written for Newsweek, Talk, Esquire, Rolling Stone, Men's Journal, Worth and Atlanta magazines. He's written four nonfiction books, Tommy Malone, Trial Lawyer; The Sicilian Judge, Anthony Alaimo, an American Hero; Uneasy Warriors/The Perilous Journey of the Green Berets; The Big Casino: America's Best Cancer Doctors Share Their Most Powerful Stories; and the groundbreaking Dragons of God/A Journey Through Far-Right America (1996) that presaged the rise of today's Proud Boys, Oath Keepers, and other violent white supremacist groups. Currently, he's working on Gowanus Crossing, a memoir of the working-class Brooklyn experiences that inspired him to become a writer.

Bobby Ezor has spent much of his life in Atlanta but is still grounded in the lessons of his Paterson, New Jersey, childhood: a fierce commitment to fairness, family, friends, and faith; a love of travel and adventure; the willingness to always go the extra yard, even when an inch will suffice. All this leavened by madcap humor, sports idolatry, wanderlust, and a fanatic fixation on food. Extra Innings highlights a very full life: Bobby is now a grandfather, always the loving husband and father, but in many ways, the same zany guy hiding in the rough wearing #7 pinstripes when Mickey Mantle, his lifelong idol, comes trundling by. And Bobby can't wait to shout "Hello!"

Barry Blitt, cartoonist and an illustrator, has contributed to The New Yorker since 1992. In 2020, he won the Pulitzer Prize for editorial cartooning.

Sergio Waksman, book designer, digital illustrator.

*Asterisk derives its name from the Ancient Greek "asteriskos" meaning "little star."

First Edition

© 2021 Bobby Ezor

All rights reserved. No part of this publication may be reproduced or transmitted in any form or by any means, electronic or mechanical, including photocopy, recording, or any other storage and retrieval system without prior permission in writing from the publisher.

ISBN: 978-1-7369984-3-4

Printed in the United States of America

Publisher: Stampa di Toro

Cover: Barry Blitt

Design: Sergio Waksman

Atlanta, Georgia

www.ingramcontent.com/pod-product-compliance
Lightning Source LLC
Chambersburg PA
CBHW042040200426
43209CB00060B/1705